Travelers of the Cold

SLED DOGS OF THE FAR NORTH

DOMINIQUE CELLURA

Alaska Northwest Books™

Anchorage • Seattle

For Edward, Carol, and Camille

Acknowledgments

I would like to thank all of those who made this book possible through their support by whatever means, before or during my research in Alaska. I extend my gratitude also to those who afterward gave generously of their time, introducing me to acquaintances in fields so varied they would be impossible to enumerate here.

The key persons are:

Maurice Siégel, director and founder of *VSD*, whose memory I honor;

Jean-Pierre Robert, chief editor of this book, who showed me his confidence from the very inception of the project, and throughout the various circumstances leading to its completion;

Isabelle Bich de Dufourcq and Claude François, press photographers and travel companions, without whom the cold and difficult circumstances would have been insurmountable;

Bertrand Dubois, gypsy of the ocean and vagabond of the poles, who inspired me with his passion for the Arctic;

Gene, Orville, and Deanna Gilman, my Alaskan family, who opened not only their door to me, but the doors of everyone who could meet the needs of the project;

the pilots of Alaska Air Guides, whom we asked to take off, land, and wait under conditions that were at the very limits of good judgment;

Dominique Grandjean, the most bitten of Iditarod veterinarians, whose knowledge of polar dogs commands my admiration;

André Bendjebbar, professor and historian, who, better than I, knows how to take off and find a trail in the deepest archives in any library.

Finally, I wish to thank my publisher, Lionel Hoëbeke; his kindness and understanding assured that the delivery of the text never became a disagreeable task.

The editors of the Alaska Northwest Books™ edition wish to express their gratitude to the following individuals for their contributions to this book: Joe and Vi Redington, Jo Derry-Wood, the editors of *Mushing* magazine, George Rae of Rae's Harness Shop, Susan Georgette, and Bob Childers.

Library of Congress Cataloging-in-Publication Data

Cellura, Dominique, 1954-
    Travelers of the cold : sled dogs of the far North / Dominique Cellura.
        p.   cm.
    ISBN 0-88240-374-5 : $32.95
    1. Sled dogs—History.   2. Sled dogs—Alaska—History.   3. Sled dog racing—History.   4. Sled dog racing—Alaska—History.
I. Title.
SF428.7.C45   1990
636.7'3—dc20   90-438 CIP

Original design by Christophe Ibach
Design of Alaska Northwest Books™ edition by Cameron Mason

Alaska Northwest Books™
A division of GTE Discovery Publications, Inc.
22026 20th Avenue Southeast
Bothell, WA 98021-4405

Printed in Singapore

Contents

Inhabitants of the Kotzebue Sound in Alaska (on the Arctic Circle) as shown in *Picturesque Voyages Around the World* by Louis Choris, 1822.

Polar Flashback

The Beginning of Time

The earth split in two, and the men and beasts were separated by a profound abyss. Thus, in the great chaos of the Creation, birds, insects, and four-legged creatures sought to save themselves in flight.

All but the dog.

He alone stood at the edge of the abyss, barking, howling, pleading, and the man, moved by compassion, cried, "Come!"

And the dog hurled himself across the chasm to join him.

Two front paws caught the far edge. . . . He certainly would have been lost forever had the man not caught him and saved his life, says the old Eskimo legend.

The Eskimo way of thinking sees the dog at the beginning of life on earth. Dogs are found everywhere, along with the prototypes of the moon and the crow, in the legends and mythology of the Arctic. Certain ethnic groups even claim to share a common ancestor with them.

This belief is based upon a legend in which a man refused to allow his daughter to marry. He finally became weary of setting out on the icebergs alone to hunt, and thought that the company of a son-in-law might be pleasant.

When his daughter resisted the idea, he said to her, "You refuse to take a husband! Fine, take this dog. He is good enough for you!"

The dog and the young girl joined, and when she found that she was pregnant, the man decided to abandon her on an island. The dog would be drowned by tying a pouch filled with rocks to his neck.

After carrying out this plan, the man returned to his people; but the dog, thanks to some magical power, managed to free himself. He searched for and found the young girl, and from their love issued forth many descendants.

As if humans and canines of the northern regions had wished to seal their common origin from the beginning of time by carrying a hidden scar, anthropologist Jean Malaurie tells us, "On the top of their skulls the Eskimos of the Arctic regions, as well as polar dogs, have a bony structure, a sagittal crest, which is not found in other humans or canines."

Forty million years ago a common ancestor of all carnivores appeared on earth: the Miacis. The Cynodictis appeared ten million years later, followed by the Tomarctus in another fifteen million years. These were the progenitors of the various species of canines, dog, wolf, fox, and jackal, whose presence could be found scattered across the earth by about 500,000 B.C.

In Europe, the domestication of the dog would not be undertaken until ten thousand years before recorded history. Dogs were utilized by several Mesolithic peoples, who followed in the tradition of the Stone Age. Scientific findings indicate that during the same time period dogs were part of a relatively sedentary civilization in Southwest Asia.

It was not until the Neolithic period that dogs were truly tamed, notably in the Rocky Mountain region of North America and in Eastern Russia. In Russia, remains have been discovered of hunters migrating toward Scandinavia.

The first dogsleds were used some four thousand years ago in central Siberia, north of Lake Baikal. Ancient rock paintings show that the innovators of this practice were the tribes of the Samoyeds, Koryaks, and nomadic Chukchis, now known as the Tchouktches.

These peoples lived off the wildlife of the Arctic, especially deer. They knew how to make use of, preserve, and develop the qualities of a dog that was genetically predisposed to hunting. Diminishing quantities of game forced them to take longer

hunting excursions on the ice. The Chukchi dog became the prototype sled dog. His appearance at that time was fairly close to that of the present day, and bears a striking resemblance to the wolf.

Both Chukchis and Koryaks achieved a high level of technical skill in the use of their teams and equipment. Their sleds might have been pulled by as many as twenty dogs, of which two were lead dogs. The sled was equipped with an arched piece to support the driver, as well as a brake to control the speed of the team or to bring it to a halt. Most often constructed of wood, the sled could be made of very diverse materials, including whale bone or blocks of ice. Strips of leather made from sealskin held the various parts together.

No one really knows when the first humans arrived in North America. However, scientists are unanimous as to what route they took. Leaving Asia, they passed along the strip of land that joined two continents — the Bering land bridge.

Two time periods were favorable to such a journey: thirty-five thousand years ago and twenty thousand years ago. These estimates correspond to the periods of time in which the land bridge was passable. At other times the Bering Sea flooded the land bridge, as melting ice raised the water level.

The first men to penetrate the New World were Paleo-Indians. Approximately five thousand years later they were joined by the Paleo-Eskimos of Eastern Siberia, who probably traveled by means of boats made of hides.

One culture superseded another: the ASTT (arctic small tool tradition), the Pre-Dorset and Dorset, up to the culture called the Thule, which appeared in about 900 A.D. along the Bering Strait. On the northwest coast of Alaska the Thules, immediate ancestors of modern Eskimos, blended with the Birnirk culture. From Barrow Point to the lands of Peary they moved across some 2,610 miles (4,200 km) in a few generations to establish themselves as far as the north of Greenland.

Hunters of whale, narwhal, seal, and sea lion, the Thules used their sleds for greater mobility. This hunting technique was adopted by Eskimos from the Inglefield Fjord in Greenland and the lands of Baffin, and by the Caribou Eskimos living in the Northwest Territories bordering on Hudson Bay. The Norsemen encountered these tribes, but were unable to adapt themselves to the Arctic. These groups were next found by European explorers in the sixteenth and seventeenth centuries.

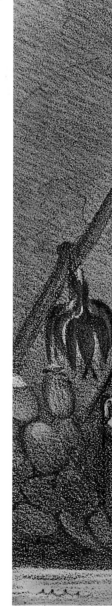

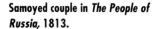

Samoyed couple in *The People of Russia,* 1813.

5

The Meeting of Neolithic and Modern

People had dwelt in the extreme North for many centuries — from Neolithic times — before Europeans discovered them. At the time of contact, the Ice Age had been over in Europe for some ten thousand years. Europeans had left the Neolithic for the Bronze Age around 3,000 B.C. The glaciers of the European plains had melted, and herds of deer had migrated north. The vast expanses of ice no longer extended beyond the polar regions; thus, civilizations developed entirely unaware of each other.

The northerly tribes, isolated in a world without trees, where the earth revealed neither plants nor minerals, subsisted under extreme conditions. They depended entirely on the animal world. They survived in much the same fashion as Europeans had during the Ice Age. They showed superb adaptability; the art of the Dorset and the ingenious tools of the Thules are the proof.

Drawn by the whale hunt and the wealth that was derived from it, European sailors pushed ever northward. The first European observers described primitive peoples; the image of the early Eskimos comes to us from their accounts. These newcomers were uniformly impressed by and respectful of one subject in particular — the mode of transportation demonstrated by these "savages."

"The inhabitants of the North," wrote H. Egede, who was a missionary in Greenland in the mid-eighteenth century, "use dogs instead of horses to pull sleds loaded with seals across the ice to their homes. They harness four, six, sometimes eight to ten dogs in front of a sled that might be loaded with five or six seals as well as the Greenlander himself. They pull such a heavy load more rapidly than our horses ever could."

Motivated by competition, greed, and passion for discovery, the whites were now in the position of having to listen to the people they had previously judged "prehistoric," since they were

totally ignorant of the methods used in the management of the dog team.

Western cultures had used dogs in war, as herding animals, and even as pack animals. However, the idea of harnessing them was totally foreign. All of the accumulated knowledge concerning man's oldest friend in the temperate regions of the earth was worthless in the vast regions of the Arctic. Horses and oxen had acquired a longstanding reputation as being the only animals adapted to the harness; now there was not only a challenge to this way of thinking, but a sudden need to adapt.

The whites, or *Qraslounaqs*, as the Eskimos called them, had already learned to watch out for obstacles in the sea. They had discovered, often at their own expense, that slush hardened into icebergs. Entirely too often their ships were crushed by the ice while there appeared to be no obstacles in their course. They had to dare to venture into the *polynyas*, channels which allowed smaller boats to pass through the ice floes while the larger ship remained anchored in a safe location.

Knowledge of the polar seas was expanded by the use of dogs in venturing from the ships. To master these animals in their own terrain, discover their habits and capabilities, as well as limitations, would take more than a hundred years.

The first contacts were made at Prince Regent Bay in August 1818. Captain John Ross is represented here with Lt. Edward Parry; they are pictured exchanging knives and swords for narwhal tusks. The creator of this illustration, John Sackhouse, is the third person. He holds out a mirror to two Eskimos, who offer necklaces in return.

Greenlanders as shown in *Voyages to Moscow, Tartar, and Persia* by Adam Olcarius.

Worse Than Eating Crow

Sir John Franklin set forth in 1845 with two ships under his command — the *Erebus* and the *Terror*. He met with death two years later on Beechey Island, along with the twenty-nine men who had accompanied him in his search for the Northwest Passage in the Wellington Canal. He is represented here by Captain McClintock in 1859, when McClintock traced the footsteps of the ill-fated expedition. From *The Fate of Franklin and His Discoveries* by McClintock.

In 1857, at Gosport, near Plymouth, the British navy had a supply center where food and provisions were prepared for the dogs of Arctic expeditions. Sir Leopold McClintock, because of experience he acquired during various trips toward the pole, was the true European initiator of the use of dogs. When he left to research the lost expedition of Sir John Franklin, he noted in his ship's log the recipe for pemmican, which was the basis of nourishment for the sled dog.

"It is made of the finest beef," he wrote, "sliced in thin, round pieces and dried over a wood fire. Then the meat is ground and mixed with an equal mixture of suet. Then the pemmican is pressed into containers which hold forty-two pounds."

During the entire expedition, the nourishment of his canine charges was a constant source of worry. He rounded out their diet with seabirds and seals, and made several frank observations about this subject. He wrote that a northern dog was capable of wolfing down several pounds of fresh meat in less than a minute. He noted wryly that it was infinitely preferable to cut up the food and spread it out over the snow before letting the team loose. "This is the only way that the weaker ones have a chance to eat, because there is no time to fight."

Every bit of information concerning the dogs was precious. One member of the expedition advised the captain not to give them shark, which caused dizziness and intestinal problems. Aside from this, they seemed capable of ingesting anything. Their culinary tastes, however, did not include crow. This was a great annoyance to McClintock, since crows are the only birds to roost on icebergs.

Harness Jack, a Samoyed, provided McClintock with wild hope one day by grabbing and consuming one of these birds, but Harness Jack was unfortunately the exception. He never allowed

his harness to be removed, and in his rank of lead dog was the protector of the pups. One day, for some unknown reason, he let down his guard; his companions on the team proceeded to devour every pup they could grab. This led McClintock to consider them in a different light, and he concluded, "These dogs do much worse than eat crow."

In fact, they showed an indiscriminate appetite, according to McClintock. Sea gulls, fulmars, dried fish, and chunks of whale were indifferently devoured, adding variety to their everyday fare. During times of scarcity, they were perfectly capable of devouring each other . . . and they didn't hesitate to kill at the first opportunity.

McClintock recounted a story that proved this point. The Eskimos accompanying him on one of his expeditions, exasperated by a female dog who constantly gnawed her harness, finally muzzled her. Her partner on the team took advantage of this occasion to bite her to the bone. So deftly was this attack carried out that, unable to howl or defend herself, the poor beast died the following morning.

Captain McClintock at Cape Herschel, as drawn by Captain May in *The Fate of Franklin and His Discoveries*, 1859. McClintock was, in Europe, the true originator of the use of dogsleds. He wrote an unpublished study of his four-legged travel companions, whose voracity and ferocity were a surprising discovery.

A team of dogs in Newfoundland, from *Arctic Explorations in the Years 1853, 1854 and 1855* by Dr. Kane. The difficulties of the explorers were not just a legend, as demonstrated by this engraving of the last century.

Nansen and His Dogs

A long stay on the ice floes enabled Nansen to become familiar with the impulsive nature of Samoyed dogs. From *Farthest North* by Nansen, 1897.

The Europeans, having no knowledge of the behavior of northern dogs, learned from one expedition to the next about the sensitive nature of these animals. The Norwegian Fridtjof Nansen showed a tremendous mastery in the field of polar exploration at the turn of the century. His accounts vividly reveal the types of difficulties encountered. In the autumn of 1894, the future Nobel Peace Prize winner described the events of an outing on the sled.

The Samoyeds came across one of their fellow creatures, running alongside the team, probably lost. "It was terrifying; all ten dogs hurled themselves against one another with the ferocity of wolves, tearing and clawing at anything that came in their way; blood flew everywhere."

It was not easy for a novice to end such fierce fighting. The Eskimos had resolved this problem by maintaining their animals under constant fear. Longtime masters of the whip, they could hit any dog on the harness, even the distant lead dog. The whip could cut an ear, lacerate a flank or anus, or take out an eye. It was a safe bet that an animal would be brought to submission with a single lash.

By whipping at random, the European explorer encouraged the hatred of the team much more than he succeeded in establishing order.

Fridtjof Nansen went on: "I sat frozen with terror on the sled in the middle of all of that, and it was a long time before I realized that I should be doing something about it."

Although he had already crossed Greenland from east to west, there were many more surprises in store for him. On Wednesday, October 11, 1895, the Norwegian wrote about how one of his dogs, Job, was torn to pieces by the team.

The dog's body, or what was left of it, was found at some

distance from the *Fram*, the expedition's ship. An "Anubis of the ice" guarded the remains of his companion, preventing the other dogs from approaching. His name was Old Suggen, and he lay watchfully by the body.

The following night Nansen failed to watch over his dogs. This resulted in the death of yet another of them, Ulabrand. Old and toothless, he was easy prey. Then, on Wednesday, November 29, it was Fox's turn. In the morning, Old Suggen stood guarding his body.

Nansen understood that to stop this massacre he would have to watch the dogs at night. This was what Old Suggen was trying to tell him.

Driving a sled team over the icebergs was a complex and perilous undertaking, and the explorers had systematically sought help from the local population. Nansen wanted to seek adventure alone on a sled pulled by six Samoyeds, and tells in his book *Farthest North* about the joys of this experience. All was going well until the team came face to face with an impassable pile of ice. Nansen knew he needed to make a half-turn, but the dogs' minds were set on getting back to the port of Khabarovo, where the ship was anchored. He shouted at the top of his lungs, without the slightest effect upon the team. Jumping off, he turned the sled in the right direction. He barely had time to grab hold when the dogs took off, dragging him across the ice, in their intended direction. In spite of his sealskin pants he suffered several snowburns.

"When I finally succeeded in stopping them," Nansen writes, "they took off again, knocking me on my behind; swearing like a madman, I vowed I'd break every bone in their bodies when I caught them."

The dogs obeyed . . . momentarily. Then they pulled like they were drawn by a powerful force toward their chosen destination.

"I managed to immobilize them by jamming my legs into the snow between the rails of the sled, anchoring it with a huge seal hook. But, taking advantage of a moment's inattention, they pulled with lightning speed. I landed on my back and we took off at a terrifying pace. I lost the whip, then my gloves, then my hat. Several times I tried to run alongside them to force them to turn . . . it only caused them to run faster, their straps tangling around my ankles, flinging me onto the sled. They now ran more wildly than ever. This was my first experience as a sled dog driver and I don't pretend to be proud of it."

Old Suggen, the "guardian of the dead." His life ended when he was torn apart by a bear, along with two of his canine companions. From *Farthest North* by Nansen, 1897.

From Wolf to Sled Dog

Soon, Fridtjof Nansen was able to note in his diary that he had succeeded in mastering his team. However, he remained astonished at how the dogs were harnessed by the local natives.

"The harness is surprisingly primitive," he noted. "A thin cord wraps around the back and belly of the animal. This is held in place by another piece of cord tied around the neck. The only line attached to the sled passes between the legs of the Samoyed and frequently creates sores."

This system effectively hindered the running of the male dog and produced an inflammation of the scrotum. This was the reason that the inhabitants of Khabarovo, for the most part, castrated their dogs.

"I was disagreeably surprised to learn this," wrote Nansen, "since upon my arrival, I envisaged increasing my family of dogs."

On the other side of the Bering Strait, in Alaska, castration was done as a matter of course, and was not the least of the suffering inflicted upon animals destined for the harness.

The Czechoslovakian explorer Ian Welzl made an inventory of some of the practices very much in use at the beginning of the century. He informs us that originally castration was only used on young wolves captured by hunters. They killed the adult animals, carrying off their young to round out their teams.

The wolf pups were carefully nurtured up to the age of four months, when life began to get complicated. Boiling water was poured over their paws to soften their claws, which were then pulled out. After this the animal had a stick forced into his mouth and his jaws were tied shut. "A veritable torture," wrote Welzl, "and the wolf howled in pain, biting with all his strength into the piece of wood."

Two months later the animal was stunned, and its incisors were pulled. Some teeth were filed, others were broken; the task

was not completed until castration had been performed.

At the end of such treatment, the wolf was no longer a wolf. He had become a sled dog and the Eskimos did not hesitate to put him with the team. If one considers that the dogs were a tool that could not be allowed to betray its master — his life depended upon it — this procedure was dictated by the necessity for safety. In this manner the absolute obedience of the animal was secured.

If Welzl reveals that dogs as well as wolves were used as pulling animals in Alaska, it is because of an early practice that consisted of tying up female dogs in heat so that they could be bred by wolves. Who knows when this practice originated.

Today, northern dogs have a dental configuration more like wolf than the dogs of the southern Mediterranean area, whose teeth are reminiscent of the jackal's.

Camp at Kalutunah, with dogs and wolves. From *Arctic Explorations in the Years 1853, 1854 and 1855* by Dr. Kane.

Gold was the reason for one of the greatest migrations of men since the Crusades. The new Promised Land was called the Klondike. Gold seekers felt they had to get there, no matter what the cost. Most went over the Chilkoot Pass, a three-month trip. They traveled on foot, sometimes transporting more than a ton of supplies across the snow. At times a dog or sled had to be carried on the man's back.

COPYRIGHTED BY E. A. HEGG
CORDOVA, ALASKA

The Gold Rush

Forty thousand men did not survive the attempt. Here, a sled carrying a coffin is harassed by a pack of wolves.

N° 551 — DIMANCHE 23 JUIN 1907 — Prix : 15°

Journal des Voyages

JOURNAL HEBDOMADAIRE
Bureaux : 146, rue Montmartre.
PARIS (1°)

et des Aventures de Terre et de Mer

"Sur Terre et sur Mer"
"Monde Pittoresque"
"Terre Illustrée réunis"

Une Lutte Héroïque
dans l'Alaska

La
Défense d'un Cercueil
par Victor FORBIN

Les chiens affolés s'enfuyaient à toute vitesse et depuis plusieurs heures l'expressman voyageait dans une fausse direction avec une bande de loups à ses trousses.

N° 551. (Deuxième série.)   N° 1563 de la collection

For some $7,200,000, the United States acquired, in 1867, a Russian colony — Alaska. Well before the first nugget was extracted from the Klondike, Joseph Juneau, a French Canadian, had established himself at Douglas Island and discovered a vein of gold. The news traveled the length of the west coast. Alaska, which was still only a territory and not subject to state laws, would draw fifteen hundred prospectors in a matter of months. By the end of 1880 their efforts would produce metal worth $500,000.

Some then decided to extend their activities into Canadian territory, and invested in the valley of the Yukon River. A dozen or so camps were set up along its tributaries . . . Forty Mile, Sixty Mile, Birch Creek. Soon a town developed, Circle City, which was governed only by the law of the miners who had built it. Claims were permitted without the slightest control imposed by any administration, and unlimited credit was offered to the new arrivals. The Klondike was the Promised Land for the few adventurers who left the Circle City area during 1896 and managed to glean more than a million dollars by mid-1897. They then owned the best claims when, a year later, the "tenderfeet" besieged Dawson City by every means possible.

Dawson City was a town of 1,500 inhabitants, where it was possible to forget about snow for only three months of the year; a town whose name wasn't found on any map, which existed nonetheless at the confluence of the Yukon and Klondike rivers. To get there, one had to climb hills while transporting as much as a ton of materials. For those who survived and didn't turn back, there was still the Yukon River to cross.

Frigid cold, crevasses, avalanches, rapids, murders, sickness, famine, exhaustion: forty thousand men never made it to the Klondike.

Among the galley slaves of the Chilkoot Pass was Jack

The book plate of Jack London, from the collection of Francis Lacassin.

London. Leaving San Francisco on July 25, 1897, he arrived in Dawson on August 30. He had already tried many kinds of jobs, and though he didn't find his fortune in prospecting, he did discover the subject matter for his life's work.

In *The Call of the Wild* especially, London evokes the daily life of the animals sentenced to the forced slavery of the harness and sled.

"Here were many men, and countless dogs, and Buck found them all at work. It seemed the ordained order of things that dogs should work. All day they swung up and down the main street in long teams, and in the night their jingling bells still went by. They hauled cabin logs and firewood, freighted up to the mines, and did all manner of work that horses did in the Santa Clara Valley. . . .

"They were all terribly footsore. No spring or rebound was left in them. Their feet fell heavily on the trail, jarring their bodies and doubling the fatigue of a day's travel. There was nothing the matter with them except that they were dead tired. It was not the dead tiredness that comes through brief and excessive effort, from which recovery is a matter of hours; but it was the dead tiredness that comes through the slow and prolonged strength drainage of months of toil. There was no power of recuperation left, no reserve strength to call upon. It had been all used, the least last bit of it. Every muscle, every fiber, every cell, was tired, dead tired. And there was reason for it. In less than five months they had traveled 2,500 miles, during the last 1,800 of which they had but five days' rest."

During the summer of 1899, eight thousand gold seekers abandoned Dawson to head farther west to Nome, Alaska. It seemed that the gold metal could be found on the surface of the sand along the coast of the Bering Sea.

Jack London returned to San Francisco in December 1897, after contracting scurvy. If his imagination enlarged upon many of the events of the Gold Rush, the lot of Buck and his fellow creatures reflected reality.

Gold was an obsession, but frequently, at the end of the long journey, disillusion was the only reward. The best claims were already taken. Tenderfoot pioneers left Canada for Alaska during the winter of 1899.

May 1900. Dogs remained the best allies of the pioneers who debarked on the coast of the Bering Sea.

Nome

Dog teams hauled freight unloaded from the ship *Corwin* in June 1907. Whether summer or winter, there was no respite.

Situated at the southern end of the Seward Peninsula, some 2,300 nautical miles from Seattle and only 150 miles (240 km) from the Arctic Circle, the town of Nome owes its name to a bit of confusion in the log of a certain English ship, the *Herald*. One of the officers noticed there was no name on the map at the precise point where there were obvious signs of human habitation. The dutiful officer entered "?Name" in ink, which would thereafter be interpreted as "C. Nome," or Cape Nome. (Some insist that Nome is simply a word of Indian origin.)

One D.B. Libby discovered signs of gold on the Seward Peninsula during survey trips that were part of an advance expedition in 1866–67 for Western Union. The effort to erect a telegraph line through western Canada, Russian America, and Siberia was abandoned, and Libby did not have a chance to go back and look for gold until 30 years later. He returned with a small party to see what he could find, arriving at Golovin Bay in the fall of 1897. On April 23, 1898, his party made the first major gold strike on the Seward Peninsula. However, the "three lucky Swedes" are credited with the major Nome gold field discovery. These three, Jafet Lindeberg, Erick Lindblom, and John Brynteson, met by accident and had only been prospecting about two months when they made their famous discovery in September 1898.

Klondike Fever peaked about this time. Many of the thousands who made it to Dawson City found most of the good claims taken, and eagerly left to try their luck elsewhere. Besides, after the Chilkoot Pass, the route to Nome seemed easy.

Three thousand men had arrived in Nome by July 1899, shortly after gold was first discovered on the sandy beaches of Nome. The beach produced between one and two million dollars in 1899, and news spread quickly of the easy pickings on the golden beaches. During the summer of 1900, 18,000 men and

women landed at Nome with 600,000 tons of freight. Their way lit by the lanterns of fortune, 162 steamers arrived on the shore.

It was chaos. Mountains of freight greeted new arrivals. Everywhere there were dogs, rations, feed, grain, and hard liquor. The crowd determined the scale of prices: an egg went for one dollar; a meal served in a tent, two or three dollars; access to the public lavatories cost ten cents.

When the flood of gold seekers arrived, Nome was about two blocks wide and five miles long. Construction of new buildings continued throughout the summer at a "fevered pitch." Those who didn't make their money prospecting for gold made it building and selling property. Most of the stampeders who arrived in 1900 stayed only a few months; others stuck it out to share in the $37,247,000 in gold produced from 1898 to 1906.

Barracks were succeeded by houses. In addition to a number of businesses, Nome counted several casinos and dance halls; troupes came from San Francisco to perform. It was the city of gold, to which everyone rushed at the beginning of the twentieth century. Nearly $40 million worth was extracted there in only eight years.

On the banks of the Yukon River, dogs haul a canoe. They worked like this every day until sunset.

How to organize a camp on a cold winter's night — a drawing by Lieutenant Back of the Royal Navy.

The arrival of a team at Fort Saint-Michael. The sleds assured the delivery of provisions to the interior. From *Voyages in Alaska* by Whymper.

Beyond the Beaches: The Alaskan Interior

Here dogs pull a wagon on tracks joining Nome to Shelton during the summer of 1908. It was called the Pup Mobile Express.

The following winter, the mail reached the most isolated parts of Alaska — thanks to dog teams.

In the fall of 1907, one Nome claim brought gold worth $40,000 to its owner between sunrise and sunset — realizing the dream of every prospector. To follow that dream now that the inlets had become overcrowded, many prospectors moved to the interior.

The isolation of the camps and villages where they settled was the source of major hardships. Aside from the fact that men, provisions, hydraulic machines and gold had to circulate back and forth, the mail had to go through. It needed to reach Knik as well as Iditarod, not to mention such far-removed points as Snow Gulch, Dexter, Dry Bourbon, White Mountain, and Otter Creek. It had to go through, no matter what the season.

Charles D. Lane and his Californian partner came up with the original idea of creating, at the beginning of the century, the Pup Mobile Express. The first railroad tracks laid in Alaska ran all the way from Anvil Creek to the region of the Snake River, and as far as Shelton, 74 miles (120 km) from Nome. Small wagons were pulled along the tracks by sled dogs. They ran the flat areas at any speed, but when it came to a steep downhill stretch, the dogs, at the invitation of the driver, piled onto the wagon.

As soon as the snow began to fall, the Contract Star Route Carriers began their relay. Their motto was, "The mail must go through!" They were exposed to a variety of dangers because, following in the tradition of stagecoaches of the Old West, the sleds carrying money were the object of robberies. Bill Duffy was robbed of $30,000 belonging to Tom Aiken of McGrath, money Duffy was transporting to the man's account at the National Bank of Seattle. Alaska, still a territory, needed heroes to forge its history. After the gold seekers, those heroes were the sled drivers, or mushers.

On the beach of Nome, water carriers devised a system that enabled them to provide for prospectors as far away as 25 miles (40 km).

The majority of dogs that contributed to the effort were hardy malamutes.

From the Nome Kennel Club to the All Alaska Sweepstakes

After the mushers themselves, there was nothing stronger, quicker, more intelligent or rugged than their dogs. People traversed Alaska by dogsled in every direction, from autumn until the snowmelt, but it hadn't yet occurred to anyone to organize a race.

That is, until the day that George Allan talked his dad into buying him a malamute named Baldy. This dog was to become one of the most famous animals of the Arctic, but at first sight, Scotty Allan hesitated to pay the few dollars that he cost.

"What do you expect to do with him?" asked Scotty, for the animal didn't appear to be anything special. He had a well-developed chest and solid paws, but not much else to justify George's infatuation.

At Nome, Scotty Allan had been nicknamed "the king of Arctic trails" out of deference to his knowledge of the canine race and of sleds. If Baldy didn't seem like a good prospect for the team, Scotty's son would have had good reason to listen to him. But 1907 was the year of George's thirteenth birthday and he didn't listen to his father; Baldy became his present.

George decided to enter a race organized by about twenty kids for the following Saturday, convinced that Baldy would be the perfect lead dog.

He had to explain to his father why this was a great idea. There was not much going on along the shores of the Bering Sea and it would be an event for the entire town.

All the inhabitants of Nome turned out on Front Street at the urging of their children, who, wishing to alleviate their cabin fever for an afternoon, would overturn the habits and customs of the Far North.

The kids, for want of a sled, fastened chairs or boxes on a pair of skis. For the 7 miles (11 km) of the race, Baldy was the perfect

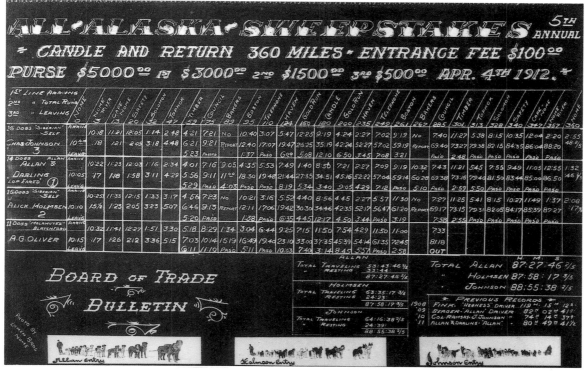

The entry fee was $100, an investment that could bring a return of $5,000 to the winner. The board shows the departure and arrival times of the mushers at each checkpoint between Nome and Candle.

Baldy, at the start of the sixth All Alaska Sweepstakes in 1913. This lead dog became one of the most famous in the Arctic.

"Fox" Maule Ramsay, who won second place in the race pictured here, imported Siberian huskies to the United States.

Departure on Front Street, the main street of Nome. The enthusiasm approached that of the good old days of the Gold Rush. Everyone capable of moving attended the event.

lead dog, and was the first malamute to cross the finish line in the first dogsled race organized by non-Natives.

The following week the participants, all very young boys, took their positions at the starting line. The number of challengers had grown, and the race became a weekly event. Before long, girls wanted to challenge the boys, and their participation was unanimously accepted. Nome was filled with an enthusiasm it hadn't seen since the height of the Gold Rush.

The adults occupied their time on clear days discussing who among them had the best dogs.

"Seven miles (11 km) is not enough to prove the courage or endurance of a team," affirmed Scotty Allan. He proposed the idea of a longer race course that would really challenge the strength of the dogs. A lawyer, Albert Fink, became excited about the project, and drew up the criteria that defined a true Alaskan dog. He then created an association for the promotion of the breed: the Nome Kennel Club.

It was decided that the course would stretch for 408 miles (650 km); then the question of the itinerary was hotly debated. From Nome to Candle and back seemed like the ideal race course, covering every type of terrain conceivable — mountains, valleys, icebergs, and tundra. It would be the total test of man and dog: the All Alaska Sweepstakes.

While keeping an eye on the organization of the race, Scotty Allan spent the majority of his time training his dogs. Evenings were spent tailoring harnesses to perfection, and on the trimming of a lightweight sled.

In April 1908, on the evening before the race, schools, banks, and public offices closed for an undetermined period of time. Weather conditions were far worse than anyone had expected, but there was never a moment's thought of canceling the race. On

race day, sleds left Nome every two hours, to the applause of a crowd happy to participate in this historic moment.

The last teams to turn their backs on civilization and head off into the bush had a distinct disadvantage. By late afternoon the wind had doubled in force and was now blowing at more than 50 miles (80 km) per hour.

After traversing the maze of standing blocks of ice along the edge of the Bering Sea, the teams had to confront an immense plain where the dogs sank up to their bellies in snow. Then it was onward to the slopes of Topkok Hill, a painfully hard climb, followed by the descent into Death Valley. The drivers, numb from cold and fatigue, bawled out orders to their lead dogs. Finally the trail twisted through the forest of the Council District.

The Nome Kennel Club had selected the race commissioners according to who could take in racers along the way. The participants could, in this way, take on new supplies and provide nourishment for the dogs. After feeding them and wiping them down with alcohol, the owners prepared beds for their animals. Sometimes racers slept directly on the ground. Others wrapped themselves snugly in their sleds, warmed by the lead dog.

John Hegness carried away the victory in the first running of the All Alaska Sweepstakes with a team of malamute crosses owned by Albert Fink. The 408 miles (650 km) had been run at an average speed of 3.4 miles (5.5 km) per hour. Hegness declared upon his arrival in Nome that he had not closed his eyes in the five days since leaving Front Street.

A dog named Sandy led the team of John Johnson, winner of the All Alaska Sweepstakes in 1910. For the first time in the history of sled dog racing, the winning team was composed of Siberian huskies.

The route to Candle.

Creators of the Husky

The winners of the All Alaska Sweepstakes arrive in Nome.

In the spring of 1909, Scotty Allan was declared the winner of the second running of the All Alaska Sweepstakes, with a time of 82 hours, 2 minutes, and 42 seconds. His malamute mixes, led by Baldy, had maintained an average speed of 5 miles (8 km) per hour, and the news, transmitted by telephone, was hailed across the Arctic as an extraordinary feat.

The Nome Kennel Club had changed the rules somewhat because weather conditions changed rapidly in the intervals between each departure. To be fair, the intervals were narrowed to 15 minutes (this was shortened to ten minutes in 1910, five minutes in 1911–12, and finally, by 1913, the sleds left one right after another).

A fellow named Thrustrup threatened, up until the last day, to upset Scotty Allan's victory. His dogs were like nothing ever seen in Alaska, with the exception of foxes. They astounded the participants by their endurance, and thanks to their sense of direction, Thrustrup, who suffered momentary snow blindness in the middle of the storm, managed to make it to Nome and stand in third place on the victory podium.

Smaller than malamutes, his dogs showed themselves to be more lively after the extreme strain of the race. It was discovered, after a bit of checking, that Goosak the fur trader had imported them from Siberia the preceding summer.

"Fox" Maule Ramsay needed no further evidence. This Scotsman and Oxford man, whose family had made a fortune in the Gold Rush, decided to charter a cargo ship and sail for Russia.

Accompanied by his friend Ivor Olsen, Ramsay went as far as Markovo, on the edge of the Anadyr River. There he managed to acquire seventy Siberian huskies, for which he paid up to $2,500 per dog. That was a considerable investment in those days, from which he expected a high yield.

THE WINNERS.
FINISH LEONHARD SEPPALA ENTRY, 9TH ALL ALASKA SWEEPSTAKES, NOME, ALASKA, APRIL 14TH 1916. TIME: 408 MILES, 80 HOURS 38 MIN. 5 SEC.

LOMEN BROS. NOME. #6298

It was claimed that a victory in the All Alaska Sweepstakes was due to three essential elements: one-third to the musher, one-third to the dogs, and one-third to sheer luck. But luck depended a lot on the qualities of the musher, or driver. The term "musher" originated in the command given by French Canadians to their lead dog, "Marche!", meaning "Go!" The word was Anglicized to "Mush!" and "mushers" was derived from it.

Fox Ramsay managed to interest his uncles in the race. Colonels Charles Ramsay and Stuart Weatherly challenged John and Charles Johnson in the race of 1910.

Finding his dogs too exhausted to give the best of themselves, John Johnson resorted to a new strategy. He placed his lead dog, Sandy, on the sled in such a way that his opponents, thinking the dog was sick and his master no longer a threat, slowed down considerably. Once Sandy was rested, he was placed at the head of the team and carried off a victory. Johnson had run the 408 miles (650 km) in 74 hours, 14 minutes, and 37 seconds, averaging 5.4 miles (8.75 km) per hour.

His record remains unbeaten, and the precedents set by the Nome Kennel Club continued to be the basis for all sled races.

A contestant arrives who will cause much discussion: a fellow named Leonhard Seppala. He covered 408 miles (650 km) in 80 hours, 38 minutes, and 5 seconds.

Of Heroes and Their Dogs

They remain forever the greatest mushers of all time: on the left, John "Iron" Johnson, whose 1910 record in the All Alaska Sweepstakes of 74 hours, 14 minutes, and 37 seconds remains unbeaten. On the right, Leonhard Seppala, winner of the same race in 1915, 1916, and 1917. In front of them are their favorite lead dogs.

Facing page
Before he passed away at the age of eighty-nine, Seppala estimated he had traveled some 249,000 miles (400,000 km) by sled. In addition to his three consecutive victories in the All Alaska Sweepstakes, he won the Ruby Derby, and earned eight gold medals and forty-three cups.

Scotty Allan won the following race with mixed-breed mala-mute-setters. Out of eight attempts at the top prize of the All Alaska Sweepstakes, he placed first three times, second three times, and third twice. His reputation extended beyond borders, and when Roald Amundsen dreamed of reaching the North Pole, it was to Nome that he wrote to obtain dogs. (War subsequently caused him to renounce his plans.) Viljamur Stefansson also contacted Nome in planning his Canadian expedition into the heart of the Arctic.

The most surprising request that Scotty received came from the French government, which in 1915 delegated Lt. René Haas to contact him. The Vosges Mountains were snowed in to the point of being impassable by horses or mules. This brought to a virtual standstill the transport of food and materials.

Four hundred and fifty dogs with sleds and harnesses were shipped, along with two tons of dried salmon to provide their food for the trip, to become irreplaceable collaborators in the World War I effort.

Of all the mushers of the Far North, Leonhard Seppala remains the best known. "That man is superman!" wrote one of his adversaries at the end of a race. "He passed me every day during the race, and I wasn't taking my time; his dogs pulled like none I have ever seen, and without appearing that he was demanding it of them. Something went on between him and his team, something undefinable, even supernatural."

It was gold that had drawn Seppala to the Last Frontier in 1901; but several years after leaving Norway he planned to embark upon a new career: "I never had any luck prospecting and I'm glad of it," he confided, "because all my friends who found their fortune at the bottom of a gold pan died one after another. It makes you think that the pleasures brought by wealth are not

The serum was carried by train as far as Nenana, where the first relay team, shown here, readied itself for departure in the direction of Nome.

necessarily the same as those which keep you healthy."

Seppala, who had learned to drive a dog team as soon as he arrived in Alaska, sold his services to a mining company. By 1920 his reputation as the fastest musher in America was securely established from Alaska to New England, Canada and the rest of the world.

In 1925 an outbreak of diphtheria threatened Nome. Children were dying. Serum had to be brought immediately from Anchorage, Fairbanks, and Seattle. The season made the operation extremely dangerous, and the use of airplanes was out of the question. The railroad could manage to carry serum as far as Nenana, where it would have to be relayed over 1,000 miles (1,604 km) of snowy terrain by dogsled to Nome.

Thus began the human drama and true story often (mistakenly) said to have inspired the most sensational of the northern sled races today, the Iditarod.

At 6:00 A.M. a phone call stirred Leonhard Seppala from his sleep. It was the governor asking him to depart immediately for Nulato to pick up the serum and return with it to Nome. "The dogs must have had their eyes and ears glued to the windows of my cabin," noted Seppala, "because I had hardly reached the doorway when they went crazy with excitement. It was like when we were starting a race in the Sweepstakes. I took twenty out of the kennel, including Togo, the lead dog. I preferred to use him over Balto this time. My plan was to arrive at Nulato with eight huskies; the others would be left at various points along the trail. They could then recuperate, to be picked up on the way back."

The people of Nome applauded Seppala as his sled moved down the main street. His journey would take him across the ice of Norton Sound, which was especially dangerous at this time of year. The first day Seppala covered an expanse of only 31 miles

The kennel of Leonhard Seppala adjoined his house.

(50 km) in order to build up the dogs' stamina for the ordeal that lay ahead.

The following two days provided fair weather. The route to the icebergs was the least taxing of all, since the dogs didn't sink in. Seppala arrived at Isaac's Point in three days, having already covered more than 125 miles (200 km). Eskimos put him up for the night, and the following night, at Shaktoolik, he again found refuge with the Eskimos.

It was still pitch black when Seppala left them to cross Norton Sound. The north wind whistled across the ice with no obstacles slowing its course. It howled across this narrow branch of the Bering Sea imprisoned by ice, where waves stood frozen in their movement. In his race to Nulato, the musher was swept along by a blizzard at his back; but on the return trip he would have to face it head on.

The following 43 miles (70 km) were incredibly difficult. The mercury had dropped to the bottom of the thermometer affixed to the sled, and finally stabilized at around −49°F (−45°C). Such a temperature could freeze the dogs' eyes as they pulled across the ice, their paws bruised, heads lowered and panting.

Seppala stopped them to allow them to catch their breath, when the huskies caught the scent of another team. He ordered Togo to look for them and soon heard the familiar growls of two dogs confronting each other, and the voice of a man calling them off. Suddenly, the voice cried out in his direction, "Serum turn-back! Serum turn-back!"

It was Henry Ivanoff, just 12 miles (19 km) out of Shaktoolik. He explained that, in the time since Seppala's departure, the epidemic had overtaken Nome. The governor had decided to accelerate the delivery of the serum by calling up a large number of mushers who would run shorter distances. From Nenana

Leonhard Seppala's team, led by Togo.

there had been sixteen involved in the relay. Seppala took orders to carry the serum to Charlie Olson, who would be waiting at Golovin.

To obtain the serum, Seppala had covered 169 miles (270 km). Now the urgency of his return was extreme. After the most difficult part of his journey he had to start off again in the darkness, facing into a blizzard with exhausted dogs, and travel 125 miles (200 km) more. "Go fellas! Let's go!"

He tried to keep his dogs in line with the route that he had used coming the other way. Icebergs frequently move on Norton Sound and sometimes mushers can go dozens of miles before they discover they are on a drifting iceberg. Sometimes, pushed by the wind, these drifting plates of ice can be forced back against the larger icebergs. It's all a matter of luck, because they can just as easily drift out to sea to melt in warmer temperatures. Knowing this, Seppala ran his dogs 90 miles (145 km) in one stretch.

After a short sleep, during which he staked his dogs, an old Eskimo warned him that the wind was gaining force. He advised Seppala to follow the river of Norton Sound. To take the shortcut across the iceberg seemed even more foolhardy than on the day before, but Seppala, not wanting to lose time, decided to take the risk.

"I regretted it as soon as the team sank up to their necks in the water," he wrote. "But the ice held and the sled passed through."

By midafternoon he made it to Golovin, where Olson was waiting for him.

Olson carried the serum to Gunnar Kaasen, who arrived in Nome on February 2 at 5:30 in the morning. The contents of the cylinder were frozen, but Dr. Curtis Welch guaranteed Kaasen that it had not lost any of its effectiveness. One hundred twenty-seven hours and thirty minutes; that was the amount of time it

took to carry the serum from Nenana with twenty mushers separately carrying it day and night. Nineteen of them traveled an average distance of 50 miles (80 km), and Leonhard Seppala more than 338 miles (540 km).

"There is one thing that bothered me greatly in this whole affair," Seppala declared later. "The record of Togo was mistakenly attributed to Balto, my other lead dog, who I left at Little Creek. In fact, Balto was used from Bluff to Nome — the last leg of the trip, 53 miles (85 km) long. Balto was immortalized, and you can see his statue in Central Park in New York, when he actually never left Nome."

In 1927, Leonhard Seppala left Nome for Fairbanks, finally settling in Seattle in 1947. He died there twenty years later. Constance, his wife, returned to Alaska to scatter his ashes over the trail.

Seppala and his dogs, winners of the Ruby Derby, in 1916.

Conquering the Poles

The use of dogs made possible the conquest of the poles. Did you say "blizzard"? Drawing by Riou.

Storm, by Riou.

At the beginning of the twentieth century, while Alaska's main passions were for gold and dogsled races, another type of competition developed in the direction of the poles. The protagonists, under the guise of collectors of scientific and geographical information, served the interests of the countries that financed them: the United States, Norway, and Great Britain.

On April 6, 1909, Robert Peary succeeded in reaching the North Pole after twenty-five years of dedicated effort. Two years later, on December 14, 1911, Roald Amundsen attained the South Pole. These two great explorers were able to achieve their goals in no small part because they knew how to join their knowledge with the storehouse of experience of those who had gone before them since 1820. Each one showed the link between the use of dogs and the success of polar expeditions.

Robert Peary innovated and put into practice the technique called the pyramid, which worked in the following way: several sleds headed simultaneously for the objective, and as they approached it, those carrying provisions (which diminished along the way) ceased to go farther. Only the lightest sleds, pulled by the best dogs, were called upon to attain the final destination.

On February 22, 1909, Peary, an extremely authoritarian man whose obsession had attracted the interest of the world, set off with 133 dogs, 19 sleds, and 24 men toward the North Pole. He confirmed later to *National Geographic* magazine that he covered an average daily distance of 25 miles (40 km). "My dogs were excellent, powerful males, hard as steel, healthy, but not extreme in any way."

As the days passed, Peary applied his "polar theorem," which earned him many critics. A sled dog pulled his own weight; when the sled became lighter, a dog was no longer needed.

Thus, by the first of April there were no more than forty

Preceding page
Robert Peary, 1856–1920, the American explorer who first (according to him) arrived at the North Pole, "to attain the glory of a Christopher Columbus." His ambition crowned by success, he came into conflict with Frederick Cook, who argued that he had been first.

Opposite page
Cook was photographed before embarking for the North Pole. He claimed to have attained his goal on April 21, 1908, thereby preceding his rival by one year.

A sled falls. The only solution is to cut the strap. Drawing by Riou.

dogs, eight per sled, to assault the last leg of the journey separating them from the pole. This last obstacle was overcome by Peary and his black servant, Matthew Henson. Four Eskimos accompanied them: Ooqueah, Ootah, Egingwah, and Seeglo.

At fifty-three years of age, Robert Edwin Peary, who had devoted half his life to the attempt to conquer the pole, was finally recognized. He had wiped out so many past disappointments, one of which had cost him the amputation of his toes, that he now savored his new hard-won glory wherever he went.

In April, as he was returning home, Peary was summarily snatched from his state of bliss. He learned that Dr. Frederick Cook was claiming he had reached the pole nearly one year earlier.

Having left on February 19, 1908, with 103 dogs and 10 Eskimo guides, Cook claimed he had reached the North Pole a year earlier, on April 21, 1908. The two men, who had participated in the same expedition in 1892, now confronted each other in the press. Peary, in this affair, showed himself to be by far the more virulent.

The magazine *Illustration*, for its part, did not seem inclined to support Cook. "The committee of scholars and specialists assembled by the University of Copenhagen to examine the documents furnished by Dr. Cook, for the purpose of establishing the authenticity of his discovery of the pole, finds his claims to be false. They have rendered the imposter, who is decidedly Frederick Cook, a guilty verdict without lowering themselves to seek punishment for the hoax that he perpetrated. No, Dr. Cook did not go to the North Pole; he didn't even get near it. And the famous snow and ice hut where the Stars and Stripes fluttered in the wind, whose photograph circulated through the press on both sides of the globe, was nothing more than an igloo on the outskirts of Annatook or some Eskimo vacation spot."

After an investigation of the claims of Dr. Cook, the Explorers Club of New York decided to strike his name from their list of members.

Only the record of Peary was sanctioned. That was hardly enough for Peary, who dedicated the rest of his life to claiming that he was "the only white man to have reached the pole." The fact was that Peary, like Cook, did not have a large amount of written material to pinpoint precisely the location of his feat. Thus, he had no proof, and his witnesses were unable to give the scientific verification that he so desperately needed.

The pressure of the ice.
Drawing by Riou.

The Southern
Polar Cap

Climbing the broken ice floes.
Drawing by Riou.

In his book *Arctic Explorations*, the American E.K. Kane, who in 1854 traversed Greenland as far as 80° N, described the state of depression from which the dogs sometimes suffered. This melancholy, which the Eskimos called *piblockto* or *perdlerorqoq*, could lead to death.

"The mouse-gray-colored dogs, the leaders of my team, were cared for like babies. No one could ever know the care that I put into them. They were kept up on the bridge, fed, brushed, and petted at the considerable effort of everyone. Today I have lost all hope of saving them. Their illness is clearly a mental disorder such as one might find in humans. The most basic functions of these poor beasts cease to operate, they eat voraciously, lose all their strength, and fall into a profound sleep. But all these symptoms prove, above all else, that their first fits, which are the first sign of mental derangement, turn into a true alienation. They bark frenetically over nothing, walk straight ahead or in a zigzag with continuous and tireless anxiety. Sometimes they scratch at you with their claws as if they wanted to crawl into your sealskin clothing; other times they are silent for hours, then break into howls, running in every direction."

Embarking by ship toward Antarctica, the dogs had to endure other suffering, notably seasickness. This was torturous and devastating when a voyage lasted six months. Chained in the hold or on the bridge, the animals' condition inspired these observations by Fridtjof Nansen: "This is how you are treated, splendid animals who shelter us at the critical moment when we risk dying of the cold! When the moment of life or death occurs, you will have, for a moment, the place of honor!"

Roald Amundsen knew that the success of his expedition depended upon the condition of the dogs. He had built on the *Fram* a false bridge to protect them from the heat, and even

The English explorer Ernest Shackleton aboard the *Nimrod*. He discovered the Beardmore Glacier, named after the industrialist who supported him in his expedition to the South Pole — which failed. Nonetheless, Edward VII decided to confer nobility upon Shackleton. He had planted the British flag only 97 nautical miles from his final destination. Although he is photographed here in the company of dogs, he much preferred Manchurian ponies.

treated them to the company of a canary to distract them. One man was in charge of taking care of every 10 dogs. Even though 2 dogs inadvertently fell overboard rounding the Cape of Good Hope, there were 97 who departed and 117 upon arrival. On January 14, 1911, Amundsen's ship came into view of the continent of Antarctica. They were not to set out for the pole until October 19.

Although the Americans and Norwegians never doubted the ability of the dogs to take them one day to the poles, the British showed themselves to be far more skeptical. Thus, Lt. Ernest H. Shackleton, in an article published by *National Geographic*, didn't hesitate to publicly express doubt about their usefulness.

"The dogs did not perform satisfactorily on the Ross Barrier, and I don't care to wait for them to do better." He went on with elaborate praise for ponies. "I had confidence, however, in the fact that my sturdy ponies, used in northern China and Manchuria, would be very useful if one could deliver them onto the ice in good condition. . . . They were accustomed to pulling heavy loads at very low temperatures."

Robert Falcon Scott was one of his followers. They had together surveyed vast expanses of ice, participated in the expedition of the *Discovery*, and traversed the length of the Victoria Mountains. Thus, it was not surprising to read from the pen of Scott in 1909: "Compared to the dog, a pony is a far more useful animal; one pony can do the work of ten dogs."

En route to the South Pole, Amundsen and his dogs came across Scott before the final assault, at approximately 90° S. The Norwegian offered Scott's party hospitality, and, realizing that the error by the British in overestimating the ponies could turn into tragedy, he proposed that they join him.

"I invited them to stay with us and take advantage of our

Among the torments the dogs had to suffer during their voyage to Antarctica was seasickness, which no explorer knew how to alleviate. Amundsen tried to distract them from their suffering with a canary.

dogs," he wrote in *Amundsen by Himself.* "The stubborn Briton preferred to trust his tracked vehicle by Citroën. And he continued to believe in his Shetland ponies, to whom he linked his fate. How in the world did he not realize that these animals are herbivores, and that the polar world is barren of vegetation? Rather than pemmican, he had carried 'finnegran,' a mixture of hay and oats, both foodstuffs which are cumbersome to transport. And how is it Scott never noticed that the weight per square inch of pony is four times that of a dog?"

Without a doubt, the British, for reasons of dietary taboos, refused to consider the possibility of having to eat dog meat. This is what all of the explorers were forced to do in times of dire necessity. Amundsen, from 85°30' S latitude, had been forced to do likewise.

The five men of Amundsen's party, with two sleds and eleven dogs, managed to reach their base, Framheim, by January 17, 1912. It was the end of a journey of nearly 1,865 miles (3,000 km) covered in ninety-nine days. Their daily average distance of 28 miles (45 km) had brought them victory over the pole while the British still labored, suffering from hunger and fatigue. The ponies were dead, and the tracked vehicles broken.

In Amundsen's book, *My Life as an Explorer,* he says: "Scott and his companions died on their return from the Pole, not *from broken hearts* over our earlier arrival, *but from actual starvation,* because of their inability to provide adequately for food on the return trip. This difference between the two expeditions was exactly the difference between dogs and other means of transportation."

The success of Amundsen displeased the British. During a reception in his honor given by the Royal Geographic Society, under the presidency of Lord Curzon, the latter was irritated by the fact that the dogs had given such an edge to the Norwegian victory. Wishing to lash out at the ego of the explorer, he finished his speech with these words: "Therefore, I propose three cheers for the dogs."

It took a hundred years of exploration and sacrifice to conquer the North Pole. Here, Peary is portrayed with his expedition in 1907.

The Polar Adventure Continues

Arriving at the South Pole in 1912, Scott and his companions found this message left by Roald Amundsen: "Dear Commander Scott, since you will probably be the first to arrive here after us, would you please send the attached letter to King Haakon VII? If you are able to use any of the equipment in the tent, do not hesitate to help yourselves. With best wishes, I wish you a good return trip. Sincerely yours. Signed: R.A." None of the men photographed here survived the blizzard and famine.

The poles were conquered. The North would take a hundred years to explore; the South would take only ten. The price of these two victories: the tragedies that marked the routes through the cold. In the Arctic, to mention only a few, were the sailors of the *Terror* and the *Erebus*, Captain Crozier, as well as the members of the expedition of Sir John Franklin, all of whom died of starvation. Some were found frozen in the ice. The American Adolphus Greely, arch-rival of Peary, and his companions were forced to nourish themselves from frozen cadavers after discovering Murray Island and surviving two winters on the icebergs.

"Nowhere else," wrote Nansen, "have we progressed so slowly, nowhere else has each step given us such anguish, privation, and suffering, and certainly no other place has brought so little material advantage."

In Antarctica, Capt. Robert Falcon Scott, Capt. Oates, Lt. Bowers, Adj. Evans, and Dr. Wilson met with horrible deaths. Many a life was sacrificed even after the proclamation of Sir John Barrow, "Knowledge is power."

They explored for God and country, even if personal ambition showed itself in each undertaking.

Still, exploration was much more than that. "It is the physical expression of an intellectual passion," thought Apsley Cherry-Garrard, friend of Robert F. Scott. That is why the polar adventure continued, with new methods.

En route for the North.

Of Sleds and Men

Why Sleds?

Everywhere in the North — or almost everywhere — the snowmobile has taken over the job of the dogsled. This is true for Eskimos as well as other residents. However, certain independent spirits prefer the traditional mode of transportation to all others: it never has mechanical failures.

On February 21, 1924, for the first time in Alaska, the mail left Fairbanks by airplane. It was a De Havilland. Its pilot: Carl "Ben" Eielson. Its destination: McGrath.

Today, the village of McGrath boasts just over 500 inhabitants. Many are Upper Kuskokwim Athabascan Indians; others are descendants of gold rush settlers who arrived in the area during the early 1900s.

Gathering in McGuire's Tavern to warm up, local hunters and trappers sit and watch the airplanes take off and land at the airport just outside the window. Winters are cold in McGrath — temperatures dip well below zero with regularity. Sometimes it's so cold the planes can't fly.

In 1963, Savoonga, a remote village on Saint Lawrence Island, was the only remaining village to receive mail by sled. The man who performed this task was named Ta-pa'-ah-mi, but the civil service and the employees of the U.S. Mail preferred to call him Chester Noongwook. It seems like such a long time ago.

When the customers leave McGuire's Tavern in McGrath, they go out and climb on their snowmobiles to check their traps. These snowmobiles can do 94 miles (150 km) per hour, and there are clients that the owner of McGuire's never sees again because ice breaks more easily under the weight of an engine than of a dog team. Because machines break down, too. And because, after all, you can't eat a carburetor.

Facing page
Cords made of caribou hide ensure the rigidity of the sled.

Preceding pages
The travelers of the cold regions pass through a landscape of ice and light.

Facing page
The igloo is still the best shelter for men who have gone to hunt for several weeks.

Twilight

Fishing (*below*) and hunting (*above*) in winter. The walrus betrays his presence to the hunter by the air he exhales when he comes to breathe at the surface. He is harpooned and carried back to the village, where he provides food for several families.

Beyond the Arctic Circle flourish oil rigs and their flares, military installations and arsenals, and routes that utilize either helicopters or cargo planes. In the midst of this constant din one finds abandoned barrels, broken-down machines, and forgotten tools. Today, extreme climatic conditions no longer hold the non-Natives at bay. On the contrary, the glacial expanses of the Arctic as well as the Antarctic have become sites of strategic and economic rivalry. In a place that is nearly devoid of men, the array of military materiel is surprising.

The Kola Peninsula in the northwestern Soviet Union is the site of one of the world's largest naval bases. Under the ice can be found an armada of nuclear submarines. The more advanced technology grows, the more natural places suffer. After the nuclear cloud of Chernobyl passed over, the Laplanders, who lived off caribou, had to sacrifice this way of life to begin raising ranch mink.

The explorers created the maps, and the missionaries, by means of sled, propagated their faiths to the detriment of the Native religions; finally the industrial nations colonized.

The Arctic today provides the Soviet Union with 73 percent of its minerals, 65 percent of its oil, 32 percent of its gas, and 30 percent of its wood. Alaska's Prudhoe Bay produces nearly 25 percent of all U.S. oil production.

The Far North is a necessary passageway: the maritime route between London and Tokyo is 11,135 miles (17,920 km). By comparison, it is only 6,462 miles (10,400 km) by the route along the polar ice cap. In October 1987, Mikhail Gorbachev, secretary general of the Communist Party of the Soviet Union, proposed the opening of a direct route between Europe and the Far East via Murmansk.

In the Far North is a people without a government, whose

The quest for game unites the last nomads on the ice, and ensures a tie with the team.

tradition dictates that its lands, and especially its hunting grounds, belong to the community. From Greenland to Siberia, through Canada across the northernmost lands in North America, the Inuit lived for many generations without borders, pipelines, or any idea of individual property.

In 1977, these people gathered for the first time in a circumpolar conference in Barrow, Alaska. They voted to call themselves Inuit, and they have demanded since that time the right of consultation, outside of financial rights already acquired, in the use of any lands their ancestors traversed. Twenty thousand years of habitation on these lands, they estimate, confers legitimacy to their claims. The ICC (Inuit Circumpolar Conference) is an international organization whose strength and influence is growing. It is active in a committee of the United Nations Human Rights Commission that is working on an international agreement on the rights of indigenous peoples.

Although the Inuit have participated in and received benefits from oil exploration and development, they are still actively working to preserve their rituals, their beliefs, their languages, their arts and crafts, their hunting grounds — and notably their right to kill whales. When the *inukshuit*, the blocks of stone piled up to three yards high, disappear — shattered markers of the old trails — they will know their traditional society is condemned to oblivion.

Following pages
A walrus is cut up under the attentive stare of a team, to which a few paltry morsels will be granted.

Some people of the North continue to travel by dogsled.

59

As Long As There Are Dogs

When the sled is definitely replaced by the snowmobile, the dogs, around which Eskimo social life partially revolves, will lose the qualities of their breed. They will remain tied up for longer periods of time. Their sense of smell will weaken; disoriented by the fumes of kerosene, they will no longer be able to detect the odor of wild animals. Eskimo dogs yap or howl, reminiscent of their wolf origins, but do not bark. Their means of communication with the team, by sound or expression or posture, will diminish. The deeply rooted sense of hierarchy in the team will disappear.

With machines, Eskimos are less likely to use their normal foresight. They might set off in makeshift snowmobiles that are poorly maintained, without food, materials for survival, extra fuel, or parts. In former days the dogs protected their masters from many hazards.

Emmitt Peters of Ruby, Alaska, knows that he owes his life to his lead dog, Nugget. She was an exceptional leader, who probably would have led the team up a pine tree if her musher had asked her nicely. Peters was crossing a river when the ice cracked under his feet. He sank in up to his middle and, miraculously, his feet came to rest on a beaver lodge. All he could do was stay in that position, for each time he tried to pull himself out with his arms the ice cracked a little more around him. He called to Nugget, who was at the head of the team. She turned in her tracks and brought the sled back into a position where her owner could grab it. Then, at his order, she and the other dogs pulled. Only a few months later, Nugget was run over by a car.

Facing page
Reflections in a blue eye.

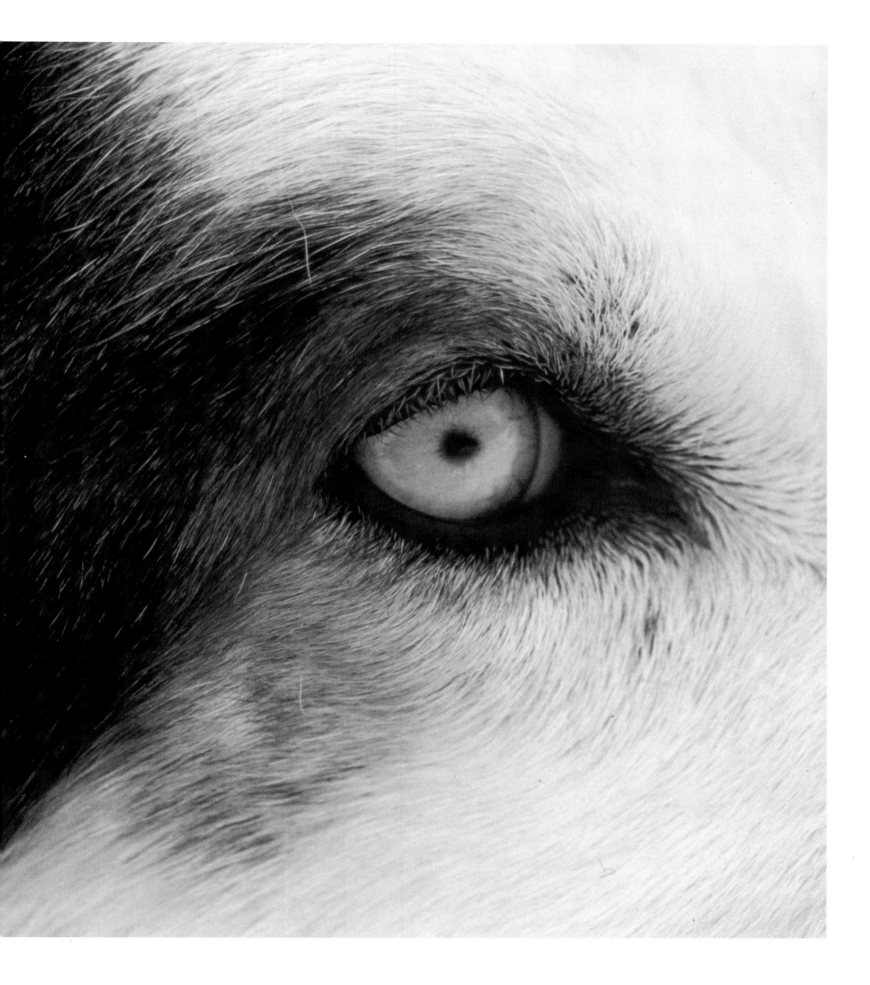

What Has Become of the "Snowshoe Netters"?

The haunting cry of the polar dog, a howl that becomes lost in the vastness.

Askimew. This term from the Montagnais Indians, which means "snowshoe netters," is credited as the ultimate origin of the name Eskimo. The Inuit Circumpolar Conference of 1977 officially adopted Inuit as a designation for all Eskimos. This term encompasses the entirety of their ethnic group, and is more widely known than any other name in the polar world, particularly east of the Canadian Arctic. Their language has transformed the word bit by bit. "Inuit" has become "Inuvialuit" in the MacKenzie delta, "Inupiat" in Alaska, and "Yup'ik" along the shores of the Bering Sea.

There are only about two thousand of these people who live in the region of the Siberian rivers near the peninsula of the Chukchis. The other Inuit, numbering about 80,000, spread between Greenland and Hudson Bay, Labrador and the confines of the North American Arctic.

Most Inuit have accepted United States or Canadian nationality. Modern machines, tools, medicines, and access to stores stocked wih canned goods have improved life for these people, who survived at the edge of the world for thousands of years. While modern conveniences have eliminated starvation and deadly epidemics, they have created new problems. As these people struggle to adjust to a rapidly changing way of life and retain the essence of their culture, the new threats to their health are stress, alcoholism, and drug abuse.

For most remote villages in the North, life still revolves around seasonal hunting, fishing, and gathering. Basketball and bingo are important now, but not as important as whaling, fishing, and caribou hunting. The Inuit will never be able to force themselves to forsake open space and the feeling of freedom it provides. They are hunters but never take more than they need; they consider the death of an animal to be a gift from nature.

Man could never have invented a more reliable way to travel over the ice, especially when a blizzard swirls over a horizon of freshly fallen snow.

In their search for game, northern hunters now use more highly bred dogs than in the past. In Greenland and the Canadian Arctic, the fan hitch harness arrangement for the dogs is often preferred, although it is rarely used in Alaska. This type of harness spreads the team of five to fifteen dogs from a single lead dog. The most vigorous animals are placed in the center of the fan; the weaker ones remain on the outside. If one dog disappears in the water the others are not pulled in after him. But in the fan hitch, unlike the harness that lines up dogs behind one another, all dogs must work harder — they are all breaking trail.

In Alaska today, puppies usually stay with their mothers for six to eight weeks. Unlike earlier times, when puppies were put in the harness at four months of age, today puppies are usually not expected to contribute much to the team until they are a year or so old. Even now, though, if they cannot keep up they are sometimes killed.

"The sled itself was a remarkable piece of equipment," wrote Barry Lopez, author of the monumental *Arctic Dreams*, winner of the National Book Award in 1986. "The sled runners were cross-braced with lengths of caribou antler, lashed to the runners with sealskin thongs. The bottoms of the runners were shod with a mixture of pulverized moss and water, built up in layers. On top of the peat shoeing came an ice glaze, carefully smoothed and shaved. The result was a flexible sled that could be sent over the surface of the snow with a flick of the wrist, and that moved over irregularities in the sea ice without tipping unduly."

After the hunt, the dogs are cared for before the owner rests. This is not at all unusual, because it is in his best interest to keep his "equipment" in top working order considering the important tasks they perform for him. They must not be allowed to deteriorate, because they are also a medium of exchange between families,

and highly appreciated wedding gifts.

Anyone who does not own dogs is not considered to be entirely a "man" or member of the race. Proficiency, experience, and social rank are judged according to the number of animals attached to the sled; a boy is not admitted to the community of hunters until the moment that he demonstrates his ability to drive the sled.

Dog mushers can judge the degree of cold to which they are exposed by the whiteness of the dogs' breath. That is the least of the functions performed by the team. The dogs show unparalleled devotion, no matter what danger is encountered. Ten dogs or less can pull a load of 660 to 880 pounds (300–400 kg) over a daily distance of 45 miles (72 km) and survive on as little as one meal every three days. Even after death, dogs have proven useful. Their skin, once tanned, has been used to make clothing, blankets, and tents. The membrane of the stomach, according to the Inuit, makes an incomparable sound when stretched for a drum. .

Long ago, when an old person felt death drawing close, he would deliberately fall from his sled. He would be buried under a pile of stones with his lead dog.

Following pages
French musher during the 1988 Alpirod.

White Men, Too

The trappers, the rugged ones who live by hunting and inside makeshift dwellings, will never renounce their sled teams for some motorized vehicle.

The wilderness is only twenty minutes from Anchorage. No more roads, three thousand rivers, five thousand glaciers, and three million lakes; this is Alaska, a land unto itself. Its area comprises one-fifth of the United States. Just over 500,000 people live there. Many have deliberately chosen a life of solitude, leaving behind Detroit, Seattle, and other American metropolises to settle into a cabin in the middle of nowhere.

Gene Leonard's cabin is open to everyone, but there aren't many people around to stop by. Before coming to Alaska to seek tranquility, Gene hardly lived an ordinary life. He was a professional boxer who had more than thirty wins to his name. Then a Cuban knocked him out . . . for four months. When he came out of his coma, he opened the first Playboy Club in New York City. Weary of working with the Bunnies — a very stressful job, according to him — he came to find refuge at Finger Lake. He bought a rifle, traps, and dogs, then set out to learn sled and trapping techniques by reading manuals. Vodka, his lead dog, saved his life twice — by distracting a grizzly bear, and later by keeping Leonard warm during a blizzard. Today there is nothing that would cause Leonard to renounce his lifestyle.

"The horizon is so far away," he says. "These mountains, forests, and space . . . although I don't own them, I have a right to be here, to use and enjoy them. And this is how it will be until the end of my days, as long as I am able to stand behind my sled."

He sells hides in Fairbanks and Juneau. Sometimes, in the bush, he comes across another team, perhaps that of an Indian couple. Then they stop and talk for a while about their dogs, or just pass the time of day. The man pulls out a pouch to share a smoke. Time has not the slightest importance. Then they go on their separate ways.

Responding to an ad in the paper, Leonard managed to

No one has ever known a
snowmobile to alert its owner
when wolves are nearby.

The choice of solitude.

Facing page
To go out with one's dogs into the heart of winter, with a concentration on the essential thing: survival.

persuade June, a woman from Ohio, to come join him in his corner of the world. "It cost me a lot in postage, but she came to share my life and that of my dogs. We have never been apart since."

The story of Jan Masek is no less astonishing. He chose the rigors of endless winter over a Prague spring. Masek left Czechoslovakia under the name of Cornelius Van Alphen, with a false passport, his face bandaged and a cast on his leg. Arriving in Alaska, he had no other way of living than to become a trapper. He married an Indian woman of Anvik, and with her help learned to go by sled to set his traps.

At night they try to find refuge in a lodge, a log cabin where trappers gather around a guest table. Here, all can eat, drink, tell their stories, and sleep, sometimes on the floor if all the beds are taken. No one would think of allowing a passerby to spend the night outdoors if he asked for hospitality. Alaska may be a rugged land, but its inhabitants have held to their pioneer values. Many enjoy their simple, solitary lives; they are open and rarely try to give a false impression of themselves. What purpose would it serve when one passes the majority of one's time alone or in the company of huskies?

Yukon Inn, Ruby Roadhouse, Unalakleet Lodge . . . everywhere you are greeted with, "Where are you from, guys?"

And the waitress lets go with a loud laugh. "Peuriss?"

"Yes, Paris!"

Or London. Or Milan. Mars or Jupiter. What's the difference, they're delighted because visitors are so rare. If by chance you are interested in dogs, there will always be one among the group of mushers who will insist on giving up his bed for you. Young or old, he will go off to roll himself up in a blanket by the fireplace and begin to tell you about the team, the cold . . . it was

Following pages
In the deepest snow, the musher sometimes chooses to lead the team.

minus fifty, absolutely unexplainable . . . or his traps. He tells which traps he uses for mink or fox, wolf or otter. When he falls asleep, and you are filled with wonder at the pale shaft of light carved out by the windowsill, you realize what silence really is.

The men leave in the morning, after having harnessed the dogs, to track game over hundreds of miles — just as elsewhere they might install themselves behind a counter in a bank. They are at peace — either they will come back or not. The wilderness makes them fatalists.

"Here," says Jerome Orville Gilman III (his friends and relatives in Chugiak prefer to call him Rome), "there is one woman for every four hundred inhabitants. We drink, smoke, sing, dance, and make love for three months, and sell our furs as if life were going to end tomorrow. Each one among us risks meeting White Death. Sweat sometimes forms a sheet of ice around the shoulders, stomach, and back . . . it always starts that way . . . every movement causes a cracking sound. Then comes the feeling of not wanting to move, to let sleep overtake you, to not think anymore. It's not painful, not at all disagreeable. You tell yourself you're going to sleep five minutes in the sled . . . only five minutes. Then you never wake up. There you are . . . every musher knows about this. But after all, whether you die of the cold or something else, the important thing is to live the way you want to, right?"

Since the age of sixteen, Rome has spent entire winters between Susitna Valley and the Yukon. He earns enough money by the time spring arrives to go to Kotzebue, on the Arctic Circle, where he buys dogs for up to $2,000 apiece. That's what Texas, his first Alaskan dog, cost him.

"A dog like this one is better than life insurance. When an Eskimo agreed to sell him to me, he could already lead a team and sniff out any danger. As for me, all I knew was what I had learned in school. That didn't help me much since I had decided to live like this, in the bush with my dogs, never seeing anyone. So I bought him. Today his muzzle is lined with scars, one eye is missing, and his ears are in tatters. He's much worse-looking than any of the dogs who follow him. But there's not one who could replace him in a storm. And he's my best friend. The time that I gashed my cheek with a chain saw, I had to sew myself up with a needle and thread. It was bad; blood was spurting like crazy. I had to talk to someone to keep my courage up, to speak forcefully. Texas was there. I think if we keep from going nuts sometimes, it's because of our dogs."

This sled is tipping over; it's necessary to help the dogs, who are buried chest-deep in the snow.

Making the
Most of It

François Varigas: his contribution
was to restore the taste for
adventure to the North.

As useful as the sled dog still is in several Arctic regions, and even though the dog comes out the winner in comparisons between his performance and that of tracked vehicles, Eskimo populations are turning over their breeding of these animals to the non-Natives, who have invented a new purpose for the dogs — sled dog racing. In the sports world, sled dog racing has sparked a continuous interest in this animal.

After World War II, a new generation of sled dog racing appeared in Alaska with the formation of two associations that sponsor the premier sprint races in the state. The Alaska Dog Musher's Association was formed in 1948 in Fairbanks, and sponsored the first North American Championship race. In 1949 Earl and Natalie Norris spearheaded the founding of the Alaska Sled Dog and Racing Association, which held its first race in 1950. This race became today's World Championship Sled Dog Race, a major event held each February in Anchorage during the annual Fur Rendezvous celebration. Communities throughout Alaska organized their own races. As the resurgence in interest in the sport spread in Alaska, it swept through Canada and the rest of the United States.

In Europe the growing fascination with sled dog racing is very recent. European sled dog racing began in Scandinavia, where the pulka (see page 153) appeared in about 1930, more than twenty years after the first All Alaska Sweepstakes race was held in Nome. The Swiss, some thirty years later, discovered the sport through the interest of Thomas Althaus and Paul Nicoud, who occupied themselves with promoting and improving Nordic racing. In 1979, France took its turn organizing sled dog races. Since that time two European racing federations have been formed, clubs have multiplied, and shows have appeared along with growing media attention and corporate sponsors.

Following pages
Trans-Antarctica 1990, the expedition of Dr. Jean-Louis Etienne. This polar adventure, which marks the close of the twentieth century, never could have taken place without the benefit of a sponsor.

Sled dog racing has captured the imagination of many armchair adventurers while others have pursued real adventures with the help of dogs.

One of the most striking exploits is that of François Varigas, whose work *Ten Dogs for a Dream* (published by Albin Michel Publications) caused a rediscovery of the breathtaking excitement of a solitary journey to the North, and the totality of suffering and commitment necessary to bring it off. His winter trek across the Arctic without radio, without road signs, was a challenge that took him to his limits.

The polar adventurer, at the dawn of the year 2000, can invest $5 million in an expedition if he wants to be on the cutting edge of science and technology. Still, the success of the venture rests upon the performance of about thirty dogs.

The Trans-Antarctica expedition, a seven-month operation that was three years in the planning, brought together the French doctor Jean-Louis Etienne, Will Steger (United States), Keizo Funatsu (Japan), Geoff Somers (Great Britain), Victor Boyarsky (USSR), and Guo Xiao Gang (China). It is likely to remain, by the magnitude of its effort, the major adventure of 1989–90. But, whatever the ambitions of the project, the level of involvement of the sponsors and the media — whether it be climbing Mont Blanc in two days by sled (accomplished by Jean-François Tuveri) or crossing the Rocky Mountains in three months by the same method (as did Alain Rastoin, Nicolas Vanier, Louis Bavière, and Gérard Sawyer in their historic triathlon) — the survival of the team, the success or failure, always depends upon the training of the dogs.

It was necessary to find a new vocation for sled dogs: the new role was sport. At the start of the race, the dogs show what the mushers call "the desire to go," charging against their harnesses in a frenzy, with no bait or lure to encourage them.

Training to Join a Team

These dogs are genetically programmed to run in front of a sled.

The dogs, in the course of a polar expedition, pull a daily load that varies between 770 and 1,325 pounds (350 and 600 kg) over an average distance of 25 miles (40 km). From an early age they are disciplined to training, the purpose of which is to force them to acquire regularity of stride, strength, and resilience.

At five months, physical prowess and disposition are already apparent in the sled dog. He shows whether or not he has any interest in running in harness either by following his fellow creatures or by refusing to run very long by their sides. If these first tests indicate that he shows an interest, he is introduced to the harness. By the age of eight months he begins to pull a "pulk," a lightweight sled. Heavier weights are progressively added. By the time he is ready to join the team, he is able to adapt his stride to that of his elders and blend in with the other dogs, accepting the authority of both the musher and the lead dog.

All the dogs demonstrate a particular personality. This, along with their willingness to work, determines how their owner positions them within the team. The result of this choice is either harmony or conflict. If the animal shows superior strength, he is placed just in front of the sled, where he occupies the position of wheel dog; this is the most physically demanding place. If he is calm, intelligent, attentive to the orders of the musher and prompt to obey, he is likely to be called upon to be a lead dog. The lead dog must also demonstrate courage without a tendency to be vindictive toward the other dogs.

The swing dog is placed directly behind the lead dog, whose behavior he watches and emulates. If a dog has no particularly distinguishing characteristics, he is destined to pull for the rest of his days as a team dog between the swing and wheel.

The sled team instinctively respects hierarchy. Should the lead dog, for whatever reason, need to establish his authority, he

stands his ground and threatens with a growl, baring his fangs with ears pointed straight up. The argument ends there if the troublemaker shows his submission by rolling on his back, paws spread, and offers his unprotected throat. On the other hand, if the troublemaker pursues his belligerent attitude in the face of the dominant dog, a display of aggressiveness will include growling with the head pointed toward the adversary, mouth open, with ears flattened and legs stiffened. Both dogs' hair stands on end but their tails are tucked under; they are unsure how it will turn out. When the dominant animal wins, the loser accepts his defeat by immobilizing himself between the paws of the victor, who then sniffs him without biting. The dominant animal then urinates in the direction of the unfortunate one, who runs off with his tail tucked pitifully between his legs.

Generally speaking, a confrontation with the dominant dog is rare. To prevent any aggression on his part, the team members resort to various behaviors. One of these consists of crawling toward their fearsome leader and licking his muzzle, after which they roll on their backs to present their unprotected belly.

By the age of four years, a dog that has been working in the harness six days a week has become a pro at dealing with the extreme conditions encountered in every polar expedition. His fur is thick, his chest is broad, and his paws are firm. He is solid muscle and the pads of his feet are tough. He is the end product of a multitude of breedings, "designed" to run before a sled. This activity is his whole life. If, for some reason, his owner decides to leave him in the kennel while he harnesses the other dogs, he becomes crazy with frustration. He howls and jumps three feet off the ground. His will to work like a galley slave to the point of exhaustion is something he shares with other beings; dogs, sprinters, or marathon runners all have the will to run in their blood.

Races run over long distances must be paced. The eyes of this dog express the prolonged effort his musher asks of him.

Following pages
To each his own mess kit . . . under threat of reprisal.

After howling and leaping with impatience, the dogs are finally free to run. Their pace diminishes after a few miles.

Submissive and dominant behavior. Few dogs are inclined to challenge the authority of a lead dog. On a team, however, it is the strongest that prevails, and altercations can end in the death of one or more of the antagonists.

Faster and Farther

The finest musher cannot hope for results in competition without "the desire to go" in the team and its leader. It is necessary to maintain that intensity from the beginning to the end of the race. Before the race, the dogs are irritated by the crowd, cars, snowmobiles, and other distractions or unforeseen events. After the starting signal, they go forward to confront fatigue and temperatures that are either too high or too low (the ideal is −4°F/ −20°C), and must endure prolonged stress. There is a perceptible change in their metabolism. The musher must watch constantly for the signals of his team, sizing up the situation, evaluating and anticipating.

The lead dog is the indicator of any tendencies, and remains throughout the race the musher's best ally. He listens to the voice of his master, picking up the tone and inflections. Certain orders provoke a series of automatic responses: "gee," to the right; "haw," to the left; "come gee" or "come haw," a half-turn to the right or left. "Line out" means to straighten out the main line without starting, and "mush," "all right," or "let's go" mean move forward.

The worst affront to the pride of the lead dog is to have to give up his position to the swing dog or any other. He has learned his job from months of training from another leader, whom he has either followed or with whom he has been paired in a "double lead." He has learned by imitation. Now, he is harnessed first and benefits from small advantages. His superiority is established most by the relationship he maintains with his master. It is to the lead dog that constant verbal communication is made; it is to him that encouragement is directed. He carries out the orders and the other dogs follow. There is little that can unnerve him other than the loss of this privilege, which would mean that a fellow creature might someday block his view of the horizon. To prevent this he tends to always give a little more

Victory depends upon the choice of dogs and their position in the team.

than the musher demands of him. And that is precisely what the owner wants.

Outside of training, victory depends on the choice of dogs; but using the very best in a race is still no guarantee of success. The variables that come into play before and after the start are too numerous to be resolved through logic alone. There do appear to be several constants, however: dogs raised and trained by their owner from the time they are able to pull a sled give much better results than do those acquired as adults. An outstanding dog is rarely sold after the age of three years. At the very best, the new recruit might adapt; however, it is unlikely that he will ever reveal the talents that his first master might have detected in him.

On the other hand, dogs purchased at a very young age will show strong traits of their breeding. Generally speaking, about half of them will be worthy stock.

The buyer will know very quickly if he is witnessing "little genetic miracles" or not. A pup who runs fast on the loose can't help but be improved by steady training. The beginnings of a great career are sometimes obvious by the age of nine months. If a dog is distressed and out of breath from the moment he tries, nothing and no one will ever be able to remedy the situation. Even the best of dogs will need several years of training to bring about the best results.

The sled team is like a chain. It must be realized that the most fragile link is the human one: the musher's mistakes are always noticed by the team. To achieve their best performance, the dogs must feel their master is in full charge of the situation under all circumstances — even when that's not the case.

Each dog in a race is the final product of selective breeding.

Following pages
Running in the traces.

The sled team is a chain: the human component should not be the weakest link.

In the Money

To transport the dogs, most people prefer individual boxes. The wait before the race should take place in comfortable conditions.

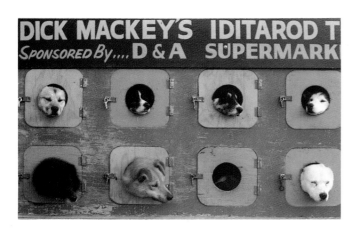

One of the challenges that confront every professional on the American circuit is to choose among the races written on his calendar — and to come out ahead financially. The number of races seems to multiply endlessly. They are generally run over distances varying between 12 and 45 miles (19 and 72 km), in three heats, from Friday to Sunday. Entries are made in races where the potential for prize money is the greatest, while keeping in mind the level of preparation of the dogs, the entry fee, and the list of competitors. It's all very simple. . . .

Very few mushers can make a living from racing alone; many raise dogs that they sell to other racers.

A hefty investment is required to become part of the racing profession. High-quality dogs must be acquired as well as at least two sleds. Harnesses, collars, beds, chains, and a van with compartments to transport the animals are part of the necessary equipment. There must be a budget for the food and nutritional needs of the dogs, veterinary care, replacement parts to gear, and the cost of new dogs and entry fees.

Sponsors invest in public notices, but competition is extreme; the hope of obtaining some of these funds is limited. Here once again, money makes money. If a particular sponsor underwrites a contestant, this allows him the possibility of raising from 300 to 400 dogs; his chances of winning are increased tenfold. He can then take on the most prestigious races, which have the highest monetary rewards: the Yukon Quest, which follows the river of the same name for 1,000 miles (1,610 km) from Canada to Alaska (Alaska to Canada in alternate years); the Alpirod, the latest of the endurance races and only one of its kind in Europe; and above all, the Iditarod, run over 1,100 miles (1,770 km). The Iditarod is by far the premier race, to be matched someday by the Anditarod, which will take place in the Andes Mountains.

The Iditarod: The Last Great Race on Earth

"Your name?"

"Jerry La Voie."

"Your address?"

"I can usually be found at the edge of the river, on the Anvik side."

"Profession?"

"I live in the bush." After a moment of reflection, "No. Write down that I live from the bush."

"Thank you. Next contestant."

They are trappers or gold prospectors. Or perhaps rodeo stars, mercenaries, lawyers, mountain climbers, Vietnam veterans . . . even political refugees.

White, Eskimo, Indian, or black (Ralph Bradley is the only black person to have finished the race), they are anywhere between eighteen and eighty years of age. They are about to face the challenge of "the last great race on earth," in which they will confront the best professional mushers in the world. All are ready to go through hell for 1,100 miles (1,770 km). These men and women (and there are always some women) will experience cold, hunger, and fear; they will cross country where they're more likely to come across wild animals than other humans. They will push themselves to the limits of their endurance.

They are here to do exactly that. But especially they are here to win.

The rules stipulate that veterinarians watch over the dogs, but there is no medical team to care for the contestants. If there is a problem, "take care of it" is the unwritten rule. It has always been this way, since the first departure for Nome. No one has ever considered complaining . . . even when Col. Norman Vaughan disappeared for two days, or when Babe Anderson became delirious after having hallucinations for twenty-four hours. He had

reached the ultimate limits of fatigue. Garry Whittemore fell from his sled; the handle pierced the upper part of his leg, and his dogs kept going.

Rugged people for a rugged land. No one has yet lost his life. So why change the way things have always worked? C'mon man! Glory and money are waiting at the end of the trail! Whoever comes in first can pocket $50,000.

It wasn't always like this.

It all began in the early sixties. Dorothy Page, the secretary of the Aurora Dog Mushers Club and a history buff, was named chairman of the Wasilla-Knik Centennial Committee. This out-of-the-ordinary, good-natured woman, with glasses as thick as the bottom of a glass bottle, somehow got the idea that a race on a portion of the historic trail from Seward to Iditarod would be the perfect event to celebrate the 100th anniversary of the United States' purchase of Alaska from Russia.

Few others shared her enthusiasm for the idea. Who would want to go to a ghost town like Iditarod — especially by dogsled? The trail had rarely been used since the advent of the airplane, and snowmachines had all but replaced dogs as ground transportation. Dorothy was about ready to give up the idea until she asked Joe Redington, Sr., who used the trail daily, what he thought of the idea.

"Sure, that would be good," he said. "But the only way to do it is to do it big. We ought to have a $25,000 purse."

There were still critics, but an Iditarod Trail Committee with Dorothy Page, Joe and Vi Redington, Al Hibbard, and Ed Carney began plans for the race. They were successful in raising the $25,000 in prize money and attracted an impressive fifty-eight mushers for the first running of the Iditarod Leonhard Seppala Memorial Race on February 11 and 12, 1967. The 50-mile

Several miles by truck, toasty warm, before confronting 1,100 miles (1,770 km) on the trail, cold as can be.

(80 km) course was run in two days over the 25-mile (40 km) trail from Knik to Big Lake. Isaac Okleasik carried off the victory in this race, and the event was considered a huge success.

The success was fleeting. So little snow fell in 1968 — a rare phenomenon in Alaska — that the second running had to be canceled. In 1969, the committee could offer only $1,000 in prize money, and the number of mushers involved dropped from fifty-eight to twelve.

By 1970 and 1971, the passion for snowmachines had reached new heights. To show any interest in sled dog races meant that you were hopelessly out of tune with the times.

Joe Redington wanted to change the tune, and he refused to think small. He saw the race as a way to revive interest in dog mushing, which was such an important part of Alaska's history, and he believed a major race on the historic Iditarod Trail would help efforts to preserve the trail. He suggested a 1,000-mile (1,610-km) sled dog race to Nome with a $50,000 purse. Many mushers and Alaskans said such a race was impossible. Some ridiculed it, calling it "the great camping trip." Many of the people who had supported the race in 1967 completely backed out. But Joe's enthusiasm was infectious, and he had a few loyal friends. In the fall of 1972, Gleo Huyck and Tom Johnson, two school-teachers, got to talking. They told Redington they thought it was possible to pull off the race to Nome in 1973.

Work started immediately. Redington called Howard Farley, a butcher in Nome who ran dogs. Farley agreed to start work on the trail from the Nome end. It was good to know they had a supporter for the trail building effort at the other end of the trail, but clearing the entire trail was a gigantic task. Then the U.S. Army agreed to help and, during a scheduled training, located and opened portions of the trail. "We even had a four-star

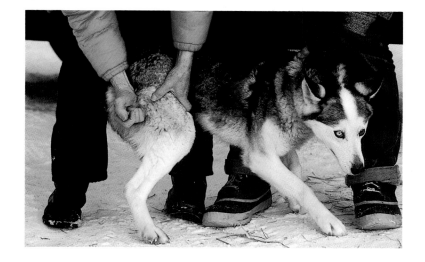

The rabies vaccine is obligatory.

Impossible to escape, and to top it all off, we have to stand in line.

They keep moving day and night . . . and start up again after a break that's much too short for everyone.

general helping find the trail in 1973," Redington said.

As work progressed on the trail, the next large challenge was raising the $50,000 prize money Redington had promised, to be shared by the top finishers. The business community was less than supportive. On March 3, 1973, thirty-four teams left Anchorage for Nome. "We still didn't have a dime in the bank," Redington said. He had planned to race, but stayed behind to work on raising the money. Muktuk Marston put up $10,000, and that "primed the pump," according to Redington. Finally, Redington and Bruce Kendall went to see Frank Murkowski, then president of the Bank of the North. Murkowski agreed to loan the two men $30,000. "That was the best loan I ever made in the banking business," Murkowski, now a U.S. senator, said years later.

Twenty days after the teams left Anchorage, Dick Wilmarth, from Red Devil, Alaska, crossed the finish line in Nome, earning the $12,000 first-place prize. He had traveled 1,100 miles (1,770 km) through two mountain ranges in 20 days, 49 minutes, and 41 seconds. No one had followed this route for forty-five years.

Nome finally had a new hero.

When prizes were handed out, Joe Redington asked the crowd if they wanted to participate in another running of the Iditarod in 1974. The response, shouts of unabashed enthusiasm, didn't leave a shadow of a doubt.

"Great," Redington said. "Now let me tell you a couple of things. The Iditarod will take place in Nome in 1974 and every year after that. It will get harder because it will be run faster, and believe me, you will never run out of surprises."

Raising money continued to cause trouble for the race in its early years, and lack of sponsors nearly killed it in 1976, but Joe Redington wouldn't let it die. By 1981, the total purse had hit

$100,000, capturing the attention of mushers around the world. It has since increased to more than $250,000. The race on the historic Iditarod Trail has also spawned the Iditabike, the Iditaski, and the Iditashoe, events that many believed were as impossible as the Iditarod Trail Sled Dog Race.

But all this pales in comparison to what happened in 1985.

The emblem that only mushers who have won the Iditarod can display on their parkas.

A stretch along the Alaska Range.

The Day a Woman Won the Iditarod

Libby Riddles.

The ringing of the telephone startled Joe Garnie out of his drowsy state. He pulled himself up from the comfortable sofa and turned down the TV before sitting back down to pick up the receiver.

"Hello, Joe. It's Libby."

"How's it going?" asked the native of Teller, Alaska. "Are the dogs in good shape?"

"Yes, Joe. They're OK. I've been at Shaktoolik for two hours. I've fed them and they aren't too tired. Lavon Barve just arrived at the checkpoint. There's a storm and quite a bit of wind. I've called for the forecast at Koyuk; the weather's not going to cooperate. But if I wait, I lose my advantage. You understand, Joe. This is my chance. It's now or never. I want to know what you think. After all, they're your dogs, too. Shall I do it?"

"Yes. Go for it, Libby. You're right, this is your chance. But be careful, just the same."

Libby hung up.

She went to get her mukluks, her sealskin boots, which were hanging over the heater. She hummed to herself while she slipped them on. When Lavon Barve pushed the door of the cabin open it seemed as though the storm were surging at his back.

"Hi," was the simple greeting of Franklin Panipchuk, in charge of arrivals and departures. "My wife has prepared some caribou and Libby left some for you."

Barve sat down, pulled off his fur hat, and faced everyone with a tired smile as a gesture of thanks. His face was weathered brown by the northern winds, but his head was smooth and bare. Along with his forehead, it had a whiteness that bespoke fragile health.

Libby Riddles was preparing to leave. It was 5:30 in the afternoon.

"Don't do it. It's absolutely crazy!" Barve advised. "It's going to get a lot worse tonight, believe me . . . it has nothing to do with what's blowing out there right now. Your dogs will never be able to find the trail."

"You'd love it if I stayed here, right?" replied Libby before she shut the door behind her.

That morning the sun had struck the snow like the glint off the blade of a knife. Libby heard nothing but the panting of the dogs, the clicking of the harness clasps, and the barely perceptible, crystalline sound of snow carried by the wind, wafting over the ground. And then the wind picked up force, gusting, then howling.

Now Libby progressed through a landscape devoid of color. Under her feet she felt the rails of the sled undulating over a series of bumps, and moving around them. The blizzard surged into the canvas tarp that covered her supplies, flapping and swelling it up like a sail so that it carried her off course in spite of the dogs' efforts. The snow stung her face, making it impossible to see what lay ahead.

Visibility was zero. She couldn't even distinguish Dugan, her lead dog. Already a crust of ice was forming over the coats of the dogs. Every few minutes Libby stopped the sled, anchored it with a hook in the snow, and ran to wipe snow from the dogs' eyes.

The same weather conditions had occurred three years earlier, in the same spot, when Herbie Nayokpuk tried to give the other mushers the slip. During the night, Herbie stayed put, and in the morning the wind was so bad he decided to turn back instead of pushing on to Koyuk. His $3,000 sled dogs nearly lost their hides out there, not to mention what might have happened to Herbie.

Libby was well aware of the story, and it ran through her mind. She pushed a button on her radio to block out the racket of the wind. After Joe Garnie and her dogs, there was nothing

Libby's choice: to leave in a storm, the fiercest of blizzards, and confront Norton Sound by night. Norton Sound is a branch of the sea that forms the cove of Nome, and turns to ice in the winter.

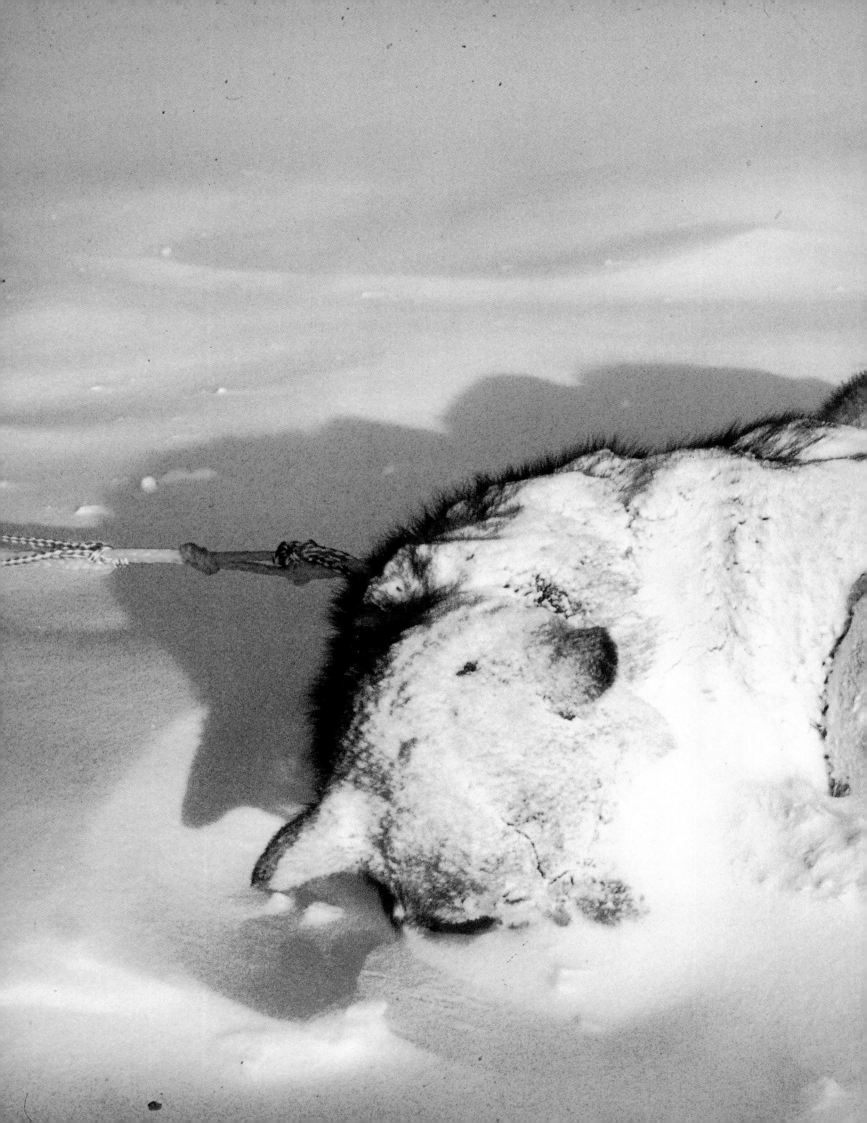

Herbie Nayokpuk, an ivory hunter from Kotzebue, a village located on the Arctic Circle. He's as accustomed to the icebergs as a polar bear. However, he rejected the idea of setting off to find Libby before morning.

she loved more than rock 'n' roll.

For hours, Dugan, at the head of the team, struggled his utmost to find the trail. Along with his companions he now tried in vain to dig a hole in the ice where he could curl up with his back to the wind. Libby had covered barely 10 miles (16 km), yet she didn't have the least idea where she was. It was impossible to fix a course and stay on it. All she knew was that she was on the ice, somewhere in the middle of Norton Sound, and the violence of the wind was increasing.

A flash of black broke through the snowy blanket that surrounded her, right under her nose. It was a crow in purgatory. Libby knew that she was closer to the coast than she had previously thought. Night fell. After feeding the dogs a meal consisting of horse tongue and ground fish, Libby emptied the sled so she could huddle inside her sleeping bag. Before she could do that, she had to remove her fur-lined parka. It was a painfully difficult job with the wind blowing at nearly 62 miles (100 km) per hour. It only took two minutes, but Libby, who had removed her mitts, could no longer feel the tips of her fingers. She huddled down into her shelter.

"It was cold and miserable," she said later. "The whole time I kept telling myself I was a fool for ever leaving Shaktoolik." Maybe she should have listened to Barve.

But, by advising her to stay at Shaktoolik, he had made Libby aware that she had within her grasp the opportunity to be the first woman to win the Iditarod.

At the control post of Shaktoolik, Lavon Barve was getting his dogs ready to go on a rescue mission for Libby when Herbie Nayokpuk arrived.

"Libby is headed for Koyuk," Barve informed the Eskimo. "She changed sleds and left one dog here. She has fourteen left."

"She won't get far," replied Nayokpuk. "This dirty rotten weather will hold her back. I know . . . believe me."

"What are you going to do?" asked Barve.

"Eat and sleep. Does that bother you? I don't blame you, but I'm not heading out at night. My dogs have got to rest. Libby's will be played out by the storm."

Barve weighed the options in his head. Here was Nayokpuk trying to dissuade him from leaving Shaktoolik. A few hours earlier he had played the same game with Libby — and it hadn't worked.

But the Eskimo might be right after all.

"Tomorrow," he thought, "the dogs will be in good form. I can easily catch up with Libby. It's Nayokpuk I should keep an eye on. He's a crafty one."

Barve pulled off his parka and sat down at the table with Nayokpuk. The Eskimo sat in complete silence. What if Libby made it through? Barve was thinking the same thought, but neither of the two men was willing to believe it. They watched each other. Nayokpuk knew instinctively that he was losing the race, and he sat brooding. In his village of Shishmaref people said that he ate crow.

The wind is so fierce that, after a few tries, the dogs refuse to go forward.

Only a few hours separate the two photographs on this page. In Alaska, weather conditions can change quickly, which makes forecasts quite risky.

The 13th Iditarod had started in Anchorage fourteen days earlier. On that second day of March, 1985, in a concert of howls, the dogs — more than a thousand for sixty-two teams — went crazy with impatience, leaping up and down in their harnesses.

Rick Swenson sat behind the steering wheel of his truck while his handlers harnessed the dogs. Swenson is a star. He has carried off the Iditarod four times. Thousands of stories have been told

about him, and almost all of them are true. Over the years his chief rivals have been Dick Mackey, whom he beat by only seconds in 1979 at the end of the 1,100-mile (1,770-km) race, and Larry "Cowboy" Smith, a former rodeo champion. All these contenders respected and hated each other at the same time.

In 1981, Swenson and Larry Smith were competing for first place. Less than 50 miles (80 km) from the finish line, Swenson tried a foolhardy tactic, unheard of at the time. He let his dogs rest for three hours while Smith was moving toward Nome. Swenson overtook Smith as they entered Nome; Smith's dogs were on the verge of collapse from asphyxia.

"My two successive victories [1981 and 1982]," he told a reporter from *The Anchorage Times*, "I owe to experience. Nothing throws me in this race, and I don't know who would prevent me from winning."

In 1985, Jacques Philip was the last one to leave Anchorage. That's the way the lots were drawn. The Frenchman slept in his car for a while, then spent the rest of the night making last-minute preparations. "This," he said, "didn't allow me time to be nervous."

To pocket the $50,000 waiting for the winner at the finish line, the contestant has to have good dogs, use them to advantage, and be incredibly tough. Beyond that, he has to get by on one or two hours of sleep a day at the beginning of the race; at the end,

A contestant may not leave a sick or weak dog on the race course. He must conduct the animal to the checkpoint, where he is taken into the care of the race veterinarians.

Facing page
After the race . . .

Along the border of the highest pass of the race: Rainy Pass.

sleep is out of the question. Above all, luck plays a definitive role.

Armen Khatchikian was lucky, but not at the moment he needed to be. After he won a televised race in Italy, the reporter asked him, "Now, Mr. Khatchikian, where do you want to go from here? We're going to help you realize that dream."

"I'd like to be in the next running of the Iditarod," Armen replied. A sponsor came forth with 100 million lira (about $75,000) for three months.

Armen Khatchikian was at the starting line of the Iditarod in 1984, but was disqualified. A year later, as his dogs advanced toward Eagle River, Armen fell from his sled, breaking his collarbone on a rock.

The trail wends its way through the spruce trees, and after Knik Lake, the progression of the teams becomes more laborious through ever-deepening snow. The dogs have settled down into a steady rhythm. As the sun slips behind the mountains in the immense landscape, the furry backs of the dogs emerge from the snow in an undulating, perfect alignment. Then as they approach the horizon, which seems barred by the dark mass of a forest of conifers, the teams appear to stand still. Now they seem to be tiny dots scattering toward infinity.

The second day of the 1985 race, at Skwentna, in Joe Delia's cabin (he is a retired trapper who lives in the hills), Susan Butcher, who had taken the lead, decided to drop out of the race.

From the time she arrived in Alaska, Susan pursued a single idea: to be the first woman to win the Iditarod.

When she settled down at Wasilla, she overcame her fear of the harshness of the rivers that interlaced near her home by

Crossing a river is always a dangerous business.

breaking the ice one day and bathing in the frigid water. In 1982 and 1984, Susan Butcher finished second in the Iditarod. Since then she had covered hundreds of miles with her dogs and they had never been in better condition. Thanks to them, she was now on the verge of realizing her dream. But between Flathorn Lake and Rabbit Lake her sled came to a halt. In the snowstorm she could see only half of the team. Suddenly she heard howls, dull thuds, and cries of pain from her dogs. Leaping from the sled, she ran to the front of the team, where a crazed cow moose bellowed and kicked full-force at the dogs. Her hind hooves struck relentlessly against Susan's lead dog, while the other huskies, terrorized and enraged, bit the animal with all the strength of their powerful jaws, increasing her rage.

Susan Butcher was not armed. She tried to distract the moose by shaking her parka, yelling and waving her arms, but it was useless. She watched, horrified, for more than twenty minutes as the moose continued to trample her dogs. One dog was killed immediately and two were knocked out. Then Dewey Halvarson arrived with his .44-caliber special. It took four shots to bring the moose down.

"I was scared out of my wits," Butcher said. "There was nothing I could do. . . I was real glad to see Dewey and his .44."

The snow gets so deep that sometimes moose, weighted down by 1,700 pounds (770 kg) carried on four long legs, are unable to move. They often travel in search of food along the railroad right-of-way that joins Anchorage and Fairbanks, but instead of starving in the deep snow, they are more often mowed down by trains. Moose also travel along trails cleared for the dogsleds. Hungry and tired from their struggle through the deep snow, they are just as likely to fight as flee. In 1985, the snow was deep, and Susan Butcher wasn't the only musher to encounter

Musher attempts to offer less wind resistance and gain a few seconds.

moose on the trail. Tim Osmar, a rookie and, at eighteen, the youngest musher in the race, escaped serious problems after meeting a moose on the trail. The same moose later blocked Lavon Barve and Burt Bomhoff. Barve managed to drive the beast off with a rap of his ax handle.

Monique Béné, a French contestant, was afraid for her life in the face of one of these huge beasts. Jumping from her sled to run, she fell into the deep snow. The moose approached her, his ears flattened against his head, hair standing up on his back; with his nostrils flared he made grunting noises. This little interview went on for about twenty minutes before he lost interest. That left plenty of time for Monique's dogs to escape, leaving her a two-hour hike in deep snow to find them.

From Anchorage in 1985, Lavon Barve and Tim Osmar led the race. Their dogs gave out just after their arrival at Finger Lake, exhausted from breaking trail over such a long distance. Sinking into the snow up to their necks to open the way for others offers the dogs nothing but disadvantages, but one of the teams has to do it.

At Rainy Pass Lodge the race was stopped temporarily. Farther on, in the mountains, a storm kept planes from delivering dog food to Rohn.

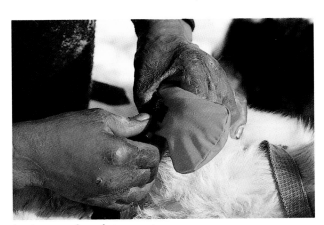

It takes rugged people to compete in these races.

This brief respite was needed as much by the dogs as the mushers. Jerry Austin, an agent for the Chevron Oil Company and mayor of Saint Michael, had broken his hand in three places when he smashed into a tree. Two of his dogs were so severely wounded that he had to abandon them. He left them at the Eagle River Penitentiary, where the convicts took care of them for two dollars a day. Terry Hinesly took a nasty cut in the left cheek, but he had known worse situations. When he was twenty-three and in the U.S. Air Force, he was diagnosed as having Hodgkin's disease. He was given three weeks, at best, to live. That was ten years ago.

At the other end of the camp, Kazuo Kojima, a Japanese mountain climber, repaired his bamboo sled. The day before, while going down to Happy River, the sled tipped over and kept rolling. It was more frightening than damaging. Alan Cheshire, a former military advisor in Oman, had experienced a similar scare. A native of Cleethorpe, Great Britain, he'd sworn he'd make it to Nome. Charities would collect money pledged per mile, once Cheshire reached Nome. But now he had a story about being chased by a moose.

"There we were, a moose right in the middle of the trail. I was the only guy with a rifle. I fired it into the air, but the moose never moved. Then my dogs ran off, so I'm hanging on to my rifle with my dogs pulling me down the trail toward the bloody moose. So I fired another one off in the air. That's dog mushing, mates."

Libby had arrived in twenty-ninth position at Rainy Pass. Several of her dogs were sick, and rather than abandon them she had decided to take care of them.

She really didn't have to make a decision. Race officials had put the race on hold, and forty-eight hours later no one seemed willing to break trail. They were watching each other out of the corners of their eyes, waiting for someone to start. Joe Redington, sixty-seven years old and the founder of the Iditarod, decided to set the example. He led the pack of fifty-eight mushers most of the day with a superb run, the team working well through Ptarmigan Pass. By nightfall he had moved onto the Kuskokwim River.

His lead dog had lost the trail. In the dark, Joe searched for the trail in the area, known for open water and overflow. Suddenly he heard a sinister, loud cracking noise. The team splashed into open water, pulling the sled and Joe with them. He got himself and his team out of the icy water, but not before his boots filled up. Only a little later, just before Joe arrived at Rohn, Pancho, a four-year-old dog back in the pack, snapped his neck.

There was a whole string of bad luck that day. Two dogs killed each other in a fight at Rainy Pass. Alan Cheshire lost a dog when its harness caught on a branch, strangling it as the rest of the team kept going.

After the Alaska Range, the mushers confront the bleak 40-mile (64-km) stretch through the Farewell Burn. The area is nearly featureless, the result of a two-month fire that ravaged it in 1977. It is a spooky, windswept place.

Lavon Barve and Tim Osmar continued to relay, breaking the trail. That was pretty much agreeable to everyone. Rick Swenson, Emmitt Peters (winner in 1975 with Nugget), and Herbie Nayokpuk (who had returned to run his second Iditarod since suffering a heart attack in 1982) were all biding their time while Libby Riddles approached the front of the pack. Lavon Barve pocketed the $1,000 prize given to the first musher to reach McGrath.

"I figure I came all that way breaking the trail out. I might as well have the money," he said.

In McGrath, weather prevented transport of food to Iditarod, stalling the thirteenth running of the Iditarod for the second time.

Many mushers were disgusted with the delays.

"I don't see why I should kill my dogs to stay in the lead, when the race keeps being stopped," said Jan Masek. "It's the sprint teams that are going to win it now. I prefer to drop out."

The race seemed jinxed and Masek wasn't the only musher to quit. Terry Hinesly gave this reason: "Because I love my dogs and don't want to see them go on suffering."

Glenn Findlay's dogs were in a bad way. The Australian saw

The musher must run behind the sled, sometimes for hours, to relieve dogs who are winded to the point of asphyxia.

In spite of the boots designed to spare the pads of his feet, this dog has endured a long martyrdom and has decided to lie down in the middle of the trail.

that they were the victims of "snowballs," little balls of ice that form between the pads of the dogs' feet, causing lesions that cannot be cared for.

Glenn had come to Alaska in 1982, riding a motorcycle from San Diego, California, on a "holiday." He met Joe Redington, who began to teach him about sled dogs. Glenn made up his mind to stay. He called his family to announce that he wouldn't be back for two years — not until he had run in the Iditarod.

Everyone was still sleeping at Unalakleet when Libby Riddles broke camp. She had allowed her dogs to rest for only five hours, and decided to take the offensive. Nome was only 267 miles (430 km) away. The last two nights had been glacially cold, at −49°F (−45°C). The blizzard was violent, and Libby's departure had

One thing every musher fears is the accumulation of snow that hardens in the dogs' paws. These "snowballs" cause incurable lesions.

Following pages
Certain racers don't wait for the sun to rise before pushing on.

Camp near the shelter of Rainy Pass, in the heart of Alaska. It marks an important point in the race, where teams are frequently blocked by the weather.

During the Iditarod, dogs may run up to 93 miles (150 km) in a day.

taken them all by surprise. She had never done anything to draw attention, and everyone, a bit hastily, concluded that her hope was to place in the top ten. No one would have imagined her in first place; Libby was so self-effacing, even timid-seeming.

When those who followed reached Shaktoolik and learned that she had left the checkpoint and headed off into the storm, some thought she was a little crazy. Others, on the contrary, thought she was extremely intelligent.

Ten miles (16 km) from Shaktoolik, Libby Riddles had spent the night on her sled, huddled down in her sleeping bag. The wind never let up, and now she was questioning her own wisdom in continuing forward. But nothing was as demoralizing as the thought of turning back. Libby checked her compass, and started the team.

She had left Minnesota at the age of sixteen, out of boredom and restlessness. In any case, it wasn't sled dogs that attracted her to the North. She used her first dogs to carry water or bring in firewood. It was her boyfriend, Joe Garnie, who, after having participated several times in the Iditarod, put the idea in her head she could do it, too. Libby had spent entire winters training his

A musher collapses as soon as he arrives at the refuge of Unalakleet. Several hours of sleep might make a difference at the finish line.

The last rush for the finish line.

dogs and her own, forty of them in all. This was nothing compared to the number Rick Swenson had bred — at least six hundred. Libby and Joe didn't have the means to take on any more. During the summers she placed wheels under one of her sleds and took tourists for rides along the beach at Nome. This was excellent exercise for the team.

She arrived at Koyuk four hours ahead of the other contestants, who were waiting for an all-clear signal before heading out onto Norton Sound. Joe Garnie was there.

"You have a straight shot," he told her.

She repeated these words to herself as she covered the last 174 miles (280 km) to Nome. The dogs were alert; the town was not far off. Signs of civilization came into sight — pylons, a railroad track, then cars. The dogs seemed surprised, perking up their ears. These noises, these cheers were unfamiliar to them. Libby felt a powerful emotion swelling in her chest, which rose lightning fast up to her throat. She turned for the last time to the trail behind her and let go a shout of utter joy.

Following pages
Norton Sound, its waves frozen upright, slows the progress of the dogs.

A Star of the
Ice Floes

Susan Butcher.

It was a day that Susan Howlett Butcher would prefer to erase from her memory forever. She would not be and could never be the first woman in the history of sled dog racing to win the Iditarod. Someone else had snatched this dream from her — a blonde, tall, slender woman with porcelain skin lit up by big blue eyes.

Susan was very different from Libby.

"She's a character," they say about her in Alaska.

A friend convinced her to go north in 1975, after securing her a job as a veterinarian's assistant on a musk oxen ranch. Susan, who had been training about fifty dogs in Colorado, where she had moved, packed immediately. She was aware of one thing: if she wanted to progress in driving a team of sled dogs, Alaska was the best place to do it. And then, she had always wanted to live in the bush.

Her sudden departure didn't surprise anyone. Her mother, Agnes, often repeated, "Susan has always been more interested in animals than anything else." But that was putting it mildly. In fact, Susan was crazy about anything that moved on four legs, dogs in particular. It was pretty close to an obsession. She had actually begun mushing when she was fifteen. No sooner had she left the Lower 48 than she had bought three dogs and had one word on her lips: Iditarod.

In 1976 the herd of musk oxen was driven from Fairbanks to Unalakleet. That's where Susan met Joe Redington. He was astounded by the determination of the young woman. (She was twenty-three at the time.) It was impossible to carry on a conversation with her without coming back to the subject of the Iditarod. This hardly displeased Joe, who decided to help her. He started by giving her good advice, then furnished her with a few products of his kennel.

126

These pups are out of the same litter.

Susan left to settle down in the solitude of the Wrangell Mountains, on the Canadian border, where she would train her dogs. She would return to Knik two years later when the first snowflakes began to fall.

She had set her sights on the goal of running in the 1978 race; she was ready. The Homestead Cafe in Anchorage agreed to be her first sponsor. Hardly anyone could resist her enthusiasm. A woman wanting to race in the Iditarod, living out of a truck with her dogs! Gosh, you didn't see that every day.

A short time after the start of the race, somewhere in the vicinity of Nine Mile Hill, Susan had her right hand halfway torn

Susan Butcher's kennel. No other in Alaska can count so many leaders.

off and ran into her first storm in the bush. She was in the process of clearing the trail, a job that was finished by a fellow named Jimmy Malamute on his snowmobile. He happened to be on his way to a funeral.

Her team took no less than thirteen hours to cross the 50 miles (80 km) from Galena to Nulato, a feat she took in stride. She said when she arrived nineteenth in Nome, "It was great. I had a lot of fun."

Manley Hot Springs Resort is an inn some 160 miles (258 km) northwest of Fairbanks and only 93 miles (150 km) from the Arctic Circle.

"Hello. Do you happen to know Susan Butcher?"

The guy behind the bar replies, "You know, in Alaska, everybody knows her. Since there are only five of us living here, naturally I know her, too. She lives about 25 miles (40 km) from here . . . 25 *Alaskan* miles. That means it's going to take awhile to get there."

Susan Butcher was living at Eureka, far from everything. After finishing ninth in the Iditarod in 1979, fifth in 1980 and 1981, second in 1982 and 1984, she won first place in 1986, 1987, and 1988. No one, not a living soul, had succeeded in lining up three victories in a row. But Susan had decided that was how it was going to be.

She missed winning four in a row by placing second in 1989 to Joe Runyan, but returned in 1990 to win again, breaking all previous speed records despite pre-race predictions of a slow race due to heavy snow, moose on the trail, and ash from Mt. Redoubt eruptions. With her fourth win, Susan tied Rick Swenson for the most Iditarod wins, but had barely crossed the finish line before she began talking about her fifth win and then maybe retiring to start a family.

Today, around her house, there are 140 kennels with a dog howling in front of each one, pulling on his chain at the slightest intrusion. There is a small hangar where thirty-five tons of food are stockpiled, enough to feed the animals the entire year. Six log cabins are occupied by her assistants from October on; there's an armada of snowmobiles and ATVs (three-wheel vehicles), trucks and four-wheel-drive vehicles.

Susan's office serves as a kitchen, and vice versa. Hanging over the stove there are, not surprisingly, pictures of dogs. Magazine covers are everywhere, and those of the *New Yorker* paper an entire wall. Susan is very much at home here in the company of her husband, a lawyer who gave up his practice to help her with the dogs and racing.

Taking a break.

Facing page
"The dogs have a language that you have to know how to interpret."

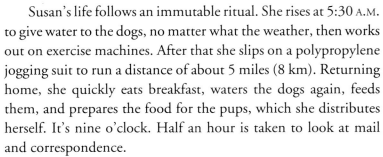

Friends?

Susan's life follows an immutable ritual. She rises at 5:30 A.M. to give water to the dogs, no matter what the weather, then works out on exercise machines. After that she slips on a polypropylene jogging suit to run a distance of about 5 miles (8 km). Returning home, she quickly eats breakfast, waters the dogs again, feeds them, and prepares the food for the pups, which she distributes herself. It's nine o'clock. Half an hour is taken to look at mail and correspondence.

Training starts at noon. Susan takes out team after team, methodically, tirelessly, until nine in the evening. When she has finished this work, she still has to feed and water the animals before she can have dinner and go to bed — and start over again the next day.

In the winter Susan uses a racing sled that she replaces with an ATV during the other seasons. The dogs basically don't know the difference, even if the engine is heavier than 220 pounds (100 kg). In the summer, that is to say June and July, her hours are somewhat modified. Taking the heat into consideration, the dogs can only run in good conditions after midnight. Susan and David sometimes leave with the dogs at three in the morning, in the early morning sunlight of the North.

This is also the time of year when Susan has to organize her promotional duties and those of her sponsor. After the first of August, she prepares for the Iditarod. It's part of her contract.

Today, Susan is also a businesswoman. She misses the days when a small plane landed near her isolated cabin in the Wrangell Mountains in the middle of winter. In it were her dogs, a rifle, a sack of flour, a ham, and a jar full of butter. The nearest road was 50 miles (80 km) away and the closest neighbor was 43 miles (70 km). She spent six entire months rarely seeing human footprints other than her own. In all, she spent two years of solitude.

At least two sleds are necessary
to start off the season: the
toboggan on the left, the classic on
the right.

His origins are quite evident. Man has, however, made of him the finest of companions.

"I believe," she says, "that I got a lot out of the experience. I learned a lot about myself, and that helped me to win the Iditarod. Some doctors try to explain my three consecutive victories by saying that women benefit from a particular type of stamina that is due to their ability to carry and bear children. Yes, of course, each time it's a physical test. I believe that if you have to find an explanation, the answer lies elsewhere. I regard myself as an athlete, and sled dog racing a sport of the highest level. During the race no one is just pulled along by the dogs. You have to keep running, pushing without letting up; it's very physical. I believe that good preparation is indispensable. When I line up at the start of a race that is going to last eleven or twelve days, my body is functioning at a level where twenty hours of sleep — and that's it for the whole time — is enough. Generally, I don't sleep at all during the last four days. It doesn't happen by accident; I'm very careful about my diet and drink neither coffee nor tea.

"The mushers of the Iditarod still take a very macho view of the race, which they consider a test of toughness, with individual accounts to settle between them in the course of the competition. They train their dogs, but many of them see no reason to follow any discipline.

"I see another explanation for these victories, and this is the main one. I take care of my dogs. They are my family. I watch them and listen to them constantly. I try to find the significance

A case of the blues . . . the life of the arctic dog is filled with trials and hardships.

Dogs and musher relax for a while.

In four months they will be harnessed to a pulk and will begin the apprenticeship of the trail.

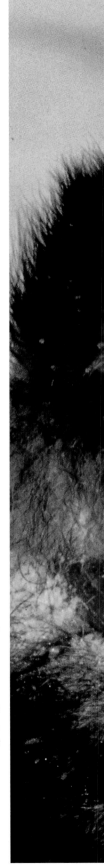

of their every gesture, to understand what they are feeling, to know which ones need to be comforted and which are doing fine. People are always saying the only thing these dogs lack is the ability to speak; in reality, dogs express themselves from morning to night. All you have to do is learn how they show what they have to say. They have ten distinct ways of barking, and at least as many howls. David and I understand them as well as they understand us. We know, for example, when someone comes to visit us, if it's a man or a woman, or whether it's a group. We can tell just by listening if a dog is angry, grateful, or if he's trying to tell us the weather is going to change. We know if a wolf, a moose, or a bear is approaching. Sometimes they growl just for the fun of it. You can believe it or not, but I can identify each one of my dogs, and I have 140 of them, by the sound of his voice. It's because I'm so close to them that I have more leaders than anyone else in this country. That's my strength. When I train sixty dogs for the Iditarod, only fifteen will not be lead dogs."

Today, animals raised and trained by Susan Butcher are among the most expensive in Alaska: they bring $1,000 to $5,000 apiece. By selling dogs and winning major races, Susan and her husband are able to live comfortably. They are the exception among mushers.

"It makes it possible for me to invest $45,000 so that I can win $50,000 if I finish first in the Iditarod. That may not make sense, but I have to do it. I mean that it's a must for me to win this race. I may be the best right now, but I want to be the best of all time."

The Boss

Rick Swenson, equipped to engage in star wars.

The winner in 1977, 1979, 1981, and 1982, Rick Swenson had won the most victories in the Iditarod until March 14, 1990, when Susan Butcher captured her fourth win. A win in 1978 escaped him by a mere second at the end of a race that lasted 14 days, 16 hours, and 50 minutes.

"This is how it happened," he explained. "Rick Mackey and I were ahead of Emmitt Peters by an hour, when we found ourselves in the middle of a storm about 50 miles (80 km) from Nome. We had stopped to feed the dogs. We were out of cigarettes and coffee and didn't have much to say to each other. It could have been a long wait. Suddenly, Rick decided to move. I followed him. We were moving at the same speed. Who was going to give the signal for the final rush, and when? We were practically at the entrance to Front Street, and neither of us took the initiative. Then, at the same moment, perfectly synchronized — we really didn't plan it that way — we charged the dogs for the finish."

Rick Swenson started his career as a professional musher in 1972, at Crane Lake in Minnesota. Lew Wheeler, his trainer, knew that he wouldn't be able to keep such a promising talent for very long. To find really competitive dogs, Swenson, too, would eventually move farther north.

The advent of the Iditarod accelerated the process.

Rick Swenson fixed up a cabin in the vicinity of Livengood, bought the first Trail Blazer sled designed and built by Dave Olson (based upon the sled used by Leonhard Seppala), then set out to meet Joe Redington. He wanted to buy the progeny of Roamer, Redington's lead dog, who had won more races than any other dog in the region.

Redington's response was positive. He had already helped quite a few people get started, with the products of his breeding

program. Swenson was no exception. He went to Joe and asked him to pick out a good female dog. Joe picked Nugget and sold her for $300. "The best investment I ever made in this business," declared Swenson several years later.

Soon, Rick Swenson emerged as one of the premier tacticians of the race. He ran each one as if he were playing a game of poker. And his profits kept growing, from $9,600 the first year, in 1976, to $50,000 six years later.

"I'm going to take care of a few debts," he said, "then I'd like to be able to buy myself an Alpine skidoo and a plane. Don't ask me about my tactics; I'm always improvising, trying new tricks. I just know two or three things for sure. You have to establish a rhythm, pace the dogs from the beginning to conserve their energy, and, if possible, continue to pace them throughout the race. In other words, as long as you don't really need their utmost effort, it's not worth asking it from them. Carry the maximum amount of food for yourself. As for the dogs, I give them 5 pounds (2 kg) a day apiece. I try to offer them food as rich and varied as possible — mutton, hamburger, beaver, salmon, honey, and cream cheese. You can't forget that a tired animal might refuse to eat what he loves best from one day to another. So it's much better to plan ahead. It's especially important to give water whenever possible. Sleep as frequently as possible, which is not to say as long as possible. Finally, let yourself go and enjoy! This is a mighty expensive vacation!"

The lamp worn on a band around Rick Swenson's head illuminates the trail in front of him.

The Father of the Iditarod

Joe Redington, Sr. In Alaska, he is known as the father of the Iditarod.

Joe Redington, Sr., has wonderful memories of his childhood. In 1929–30, years of the Great Depression, he was on the road crossing the States with his father and brother, accompanying a band of gypsies from Ireland. At that time he crossed every state in the Union, except for the northernmost territory — Alaska. Later on, he began to think more and more about it. Everything there seemed to be bigger and more beautiful, and he decided he would live there no matter what.

After serving his country up until December 6, 1945, in the front lines for General MacArthur, he tried selling jeeps and agricultural equipment for a while. Three years later he arrived at Knik, Alaska, with a sled and eighteen dollars in his pocket. He spent thirteen of it to buy a piece of land. The other five was invested in provisions to last a few days.

Joe was starting to get hungry when Providence sent him reinforcements in the form of a black bear standing on its hind legs, ready to attack. He managed to bring it down. Three pioneers who lived in the area, Heinie Snider, Fred Hurd, and Jay Levan, offered him 110 pounds (50 kg) of potatoes to go with the bear meat. Joe never forgot this gesture of kindness, and vowed to help others whenever he could.

His military experience combined with being a woodsman qualified him to apply for a job offered by the 5039th Maintenance and Supply Group. His job was to locate the wreckage of downed airplanes, and bring back any survivors or their belongings, as well as any equipment of value that might be left in the plane. During these operations, Joe used a sled pulled by anywhere from five to eighteen dogs, weighing approximately 88 pounds (40 kg) each, and soon became a musher without peer.

From 1949 to 1957 he saved many lives and salvaged valuable materials.

It was after he married Vi, his sweetheart from Pennsylvania,
that he left Knik, and his job. "It was getting too crowded." They
lived in a tent for two years at Flathorn Lake in the middle of the
bush. He built kennels for his dogs, then his own house. For the
next fifteen years Joe used the Iditarod trail every day as his main
transportation route to town. He was the happiest of men, his
dogs were reputedly the best in the country, and with Vi he raised
four fine children. It seemed as if there was not a care in sight.

Enter Dorothy Page.

Thanks to their combined efforts, they managed to produce
the last great race on earth. Everywhere in Alaska, Joe is known
today as the father of the Iditarod. He has run in every race since
1974, except in 1983 when injuries from a moose encounter while
training for the race forced him to the sidelines. Although he has
not won any of them, what's the difference? He has come in fifth
four times and is always in the top twenty. He helped Rick
Swenson and Susan Butcher become the two great champions of
all time, and has introduced many others to the sport. He has
inspired the entire country with the spirit of the Iditarod.

On the Trail of the Great Racers

Claire . . .

The Iditarod Trail Sled Dog Race captured the imaginations of people everywhere and interest in the sport swelled. Alaska's official state sport has become an international sport, and the Iditarod routinely draws mushers from around the world.

Armen Khatchikian of Italy started training with Joe Redington, Sr., in 1984 and ran his first 200-mile race after only one hour's practice. On his third try, he finally finished an Iditarod race in 1986, in forty-fourth place out of fifty-five finishers. In 1984, Khatchikian returned to Italy and began, with Redington's encouragement, a school for training dog mushers. Both talked about the idea of starting a European race. Khatchikian went to promoter and dog-lover Nicola Bovoli, who helped pull together the sponsors needed to make the race a reality. In 1988 the first Alpirod International Sled Dog Race was held, with twenty-six teams competing. Khatchikian finished in tenth place.

Jacques and Claire Philip have one of the most promising records in Europe. Thanks to their sponsor, Royal Canine, they are able to leave their home some 40 miles south of Paris for at least six months each year to spend time in Alaska, training with their dogs on land made available to them by Joe Redington. Jacques placed fifth in the 1988 Alpirod, and sixth in the 1989 race. They ran their first Iditarod in 1985; Jacques took an impressive twenty-third place and Claire finished thirty-seventh. Both improved their finishes when they ran again in 1987. Each has been Sled Dog Champion of France; they are two of the top racers in Europe. While Claire is concentrating on the Alpirod, Jacques is still pursuing the Iditarod. He finished in fourteenth place in 1988 and fifteenth in 1990.

The first European to come to Alaska to participate in a major long-distance race was Martin Buser. A native of Switzerland, Buser immigrated to the United States in 1979 because of his

interest in dog mushing. He trained with Earl and Natalie Norris, two leaders in Alaska's mushing circles. In 1980 he ran his first Iditarod and placed twenty-second out of a field of sixty-two entrants. He has finished in the top ten in the last four races. His best finish was in 1988, when he took third place.

A Norwegian, Rune Hesthammer, placed tenth in the 1986 Iditarod to win the Rookie of the Year award, which goes to the highest-placing rookie. He had leased a team of dogs from Susan Butcher after training with her. Earlier, he worked three years in a remote power station in Spitsbergen to save enough money to come to Alaska and train for the race. In the 1986 Iditarod another rookie Norwegian, Nina Hotvedt, finished nineteenth, with a team of Joe Redington's dogs.

Kazuo Kajima of Tokyo, Japan, ran his first Iditarod in 1985. A mountain climber and adventurer, Kazuo was part of a five-month expedition across Greenland that used dog teams. The sales manager for a furniture company brought a film crew with him to cover Kazuo's race. They got good footage when Kazuo crashed at their feet after a spectacular ride in the Happy River valley. He repaired his sled and went on to finish twenty-seventh in his first race.

Alaskan mushers still capture top honors in the major races. Joe Runyan of Nenana is the only musher to win the Iditarod, the Yukon Quest, and the Alpirod. He ran his first Iditarod in 1983 and placed eleventh. In 1984 he ran the Yukon Quest and finished fourth. He returned to the Quest in 1985 and won it. In 1986 he placed fourth in the Iditarod, in 1988 he won the inaugural Alpirod, and in 1989 he won the Iditarod.

and Jacques Philip.

Arctic Ocean

HERSCHEL
ISLAND

Route of the Gold Rush
via Dawson City

Transport of serum by train as far
as Nenana, then by sled to Nome

Route of the Iditarod:
Anchorage - Nome

Route of the All Alaska Sweepstakes:
Nome - Candle - Nome

Railroad

Fort Yukon

Circle

Millers Camp

Nation

Rock Creek

Dawson City

Stewart Crossing

THE KLONDIKE

WRANGELL
MOUNTAINS

Carmacks

CANADA

Whitehorse

Chilkoot Pass (elev. 3500')

Skagway

Haines

Alaska

Juneau

Douglas

Dominique Grandjean is a doctor of veterinary medicine, doctor of nutrition, master assistant to the National School of Veterinary Medicine of Maisons-Alfort, president of the Study and Research Group of Canine Sports Medicine, federal veterinarian to the French Federation of Pulka and Sled Dogs, initiator of the Veterinary Commission of the European Sled Dog Racing Association, member of the veterinary team for the Iditarod, and the preeminent French specialist for northern dogs and sleds. He compiled much of the data on international racing that follows, for which the author expresses his gratitude.

Appendix

Sled Dog Racing

For several years now sled dog racing has been increasingly perceived by Europeans and North Americans as a legitimate sport. With the impact and help of the media, a complete calendar of the races has developed on both sides of the Atlantic. Between December and April hundreds of official competitions take place in Europe and North America, an indication of specialization in this sport.

Information on North American races and organizations was compiled from data provided by *Mushing*, a bi-monthly magazine providing international coverage of events and topics of interest to mushers. For information about this magazine, write P.O. Box 149, Ester, Alaska 99725.

Speed Races

vary in length and are run in heats over two or three days. There are literally hundreds of races in this category held throughout the world. Among the most famous in this class are the Fur Rondy World Championships held each February in Anchorage, Alaska, and the Open North American Championship held one month later in Fairbanks.

Mid-Distance Races

vary from 100 to 500 miles (160 to 805 km). The number of races in this category appears to be growing. The John Beargrease Sled Dog Marathon, a 500-mile race held in Minnesota early each January, and the Kusko 300, a 300-mile race that starts from Bethel, Alaska, in mid-January, are two races often characterized as training grounds for the Iditarod. In France, the Pesse, 93 miles (150 km) across the Haut-Jura, falls into the mid-distance category.

Endurance or Long Distance Races

require more skill, stamina, and strength from mushers and their dogs than most races.

Two races in Alaska in this category attract mushers from around the world. The Iditarod Trail Sled Dog Race starts the first Saturday in March each year and covers 1,100 miles (1,770 km), following southern or northern routes in alternating years, with approximately twenty-seven checkpoints. The fastest finish of the race, achieved on the longer northern route by Susan Butcher in 1990, was 11 days, 1 hour, 53 minutes, and 23 seconds. The Yukon Quest International Sled Dog Race follows a 1,000-mile (1,610-km) route between Fairbanks, Alaska, and Whitehorse, Yukon Territory, with seven check-

points. Racers must travel longer between checkpoints and carry heavier loads than in the Iditarod. The Quest changes its starting point in alternating years, giving both Fairbanks and Whitehorse the experience of starts and finishes. Vern Halter won the 1990 Yukon Quest in 11 days, 17 hours, and 9 minutes, the second-fastest time in the history of the six-year-old race.

The most famous race in Europe is the Alpirod, which was started in 1988. In the Alpirod, competition takes place in stages over 1,000 kilometers (approximately 621 miles). The route traverses Italy, France, Germany, and Switzerland. This is the most beautiful and most difficult of the European races and attracts a dozen American competitors each year. Joe Runyan of Nenana, Alaska, is the only musher to win all three long-distance races, taking the Yukon Quest in 1985, the Alpirod in 1988, and the Iditarod in 1989.

Pulk racing appeared in Scandinavia around 1930, then in Switzerland thirty years later.

Pulk Racing and Skijoring

The Equipment

Along with the rapid growth of sled dog racing, two other sports have grown considerably, along parallel lines. They come from Scandinavia and are known as pulka (or pulk racing) and Nordic-style mushing (or skijoring).

For pulk racing, no sled is necessary. A skier is attached by a simple, flexible cord behind his dog, who is pulling a streamlined frame weighing 44 pounds (20 kg), called a "pulka." With more than 150,000 people registered to practice the sport in Scandinavia and already several hundred outside of Northern Europe, there is no doubt that this sport, the ultimate test of which is the yearly White Pulka in Isère, will soon be drawing crowds. Only one dog is necessary and the best results are obtained with hunting dogs, which are much faster than the northern breeds over the usual distance of the race, 7.5 miles (12 km). The equipment is not expensive and is practical and ecologically sound.

Across Canada and the United States, pulk racing has been slow to catch on, but is quickly gaining in recreational popularity along with skijoring. More than pulk racing, skijoring is the simplest and most intimate form of dog driving, involving a skier hooked to one or more dogs in harness. It is better known in North America than pulk racing, but, unlike in Europe, organizations and races for both sports are difficult to find. This will not remain the case, however, if talk about adding a skier-and-dog event to future Olympics becomes reality.

The sports of sled dog racing and pulk racing require a minimum of equipment. For sled dog racing, other than a special harness, collars, and attachment lines (which can be made more sophisticated in order to reduce and distribute the amount of traction), all that is needed is, of course, a sled. For very long distances, longer sleds are utilized. These are approximately 4 yards (3.5 m), with the bottom riding between the two runners (they are sometimes referred to as toboggans). In speed races, shorter sleds, about 2.5 yards (2.2 m) without cargo area, are used. They weigh between 15 and 22 pounds (7 and 10 kg), three times less than long sleds. To make them lighter and more supple so they will hold their edges in storms or on steep slopes, the runners are made of wood, Kevlar, or carbon fiber. On a steep slope a team can attain a speed of 28 to 31 miles (45 to 50 km) per hour.

The sled costs around $1,000, to which one must add the cost of a vehicle to transport it, with individual compartments for the dogs.

For pulk racing one needs only three good dogs; the investment is much less onerous. Basic equipment includes good ski gear, a pulka with a rigid pole that goes over the flanks of the dog, and a harness.

Indispensable for the racer is a container of ski wax, which, according to the condition of the snow, can allow him to gain precious seconds.

Mitts, compass, parka with fur, and protection for the face: these are the minimum precautions against the cold and blizzards.

Sports Medicine for Dogs

The competition of sled dogs is now recognized as a sport of the highest level, and is considered, prepared for, and treated as such by veterinarians and mushers alike. Thus, the preparation of the dog depends upon four factors of equal importance.

Genetic Selection

A careful breeding program can develop the inherited tendencies of an animal toward better performance.

Psychology

A dog runs because he has the "desire to go" and to please his master. To have a good team, the psychological relationship between the dogs and their master must be perfect. Let us not forget that a sled is run by voice command, not with reins or whip.

Training

From August to April, the dogs are trained according to specific objectives (speed, endurance, and resistance), with very precise programs, at least four days a week. In the absence of snow, the competitors use carts with wheels on forest trails.

Nutrition

The nutritional needs of the sled dog could be called primitive; the animal requires very specific quantities of fats, high-quality proteins, mineral salts, and related vitamins. A very high degree of expertise has been attained in this area. The nutritional needs of the best teams are regularly adjusted by computer.

One very important rule of thumb: contrary to popular opinion, a sled dog eats less, pound for pound, than the average house dog. It has actually been proven that the sled dog has far better energy output from his food. Although he eats and drinks relatively little, the sled dog is an athlete that can develop problems. In competition, the primary problem has to do with his paws and pads. The effects of the snow can produce specific pathologies such as inflammation between the toes as well as cracks and cuts. As the Eskimos say, "No paws, no dog." To prevent or remedy this problem, some dog owners use protective boots made of nylon or fur, which the dogs adjust to easily.

Another frequent problem is the "diarrhea-dehydration-stress" syndrome. The effort and stress necessary for competition, felt especially by the dog in a race that may draw as many as ten thousand spectators, can cause diarrhea. This in itself presents no danger unless it dehydrates the animal, especially at temperatures below 32°F (0°C). Mountaineers are well acquainted with this phenomenon. That is why mushers concoct a mixture to prevent this condition before the fact.

Finally, muscles and tendons are put to an extreme test, as in any other sport. To take care of these medical aspects of racing, organizations provide teams of veterinarians. Two specialists are present around the clock at all races.

The Samoyed

This was the first northern dog to be known by the public at large. His abundant white fur distinguishes him. His origins are prehistoric, by way of the Samoyeds, a nomadic tribe of the Russian Arctic.

General Appearance
Arctic spitz, best described as square-shaped. Elegant in appearance, displaying strength, grace, agility, dignity, and self-assurance. Carries its tail over its back. The Samoyed is a trotter. His pace should be quick and energetic.

Coat
Well supplied with fur that is heavy, supple, and thick. It forms a ruff around the neck and shoulders. The undercoat is short, soft, and dense.

Color
White, cream, or white and biscuit-colored. The under-hair should be white with light touches of biscuit, and should never appear beige.

Size
Males from 21 to 23.5 inches (53 to 60 cm).
Females, 19 to 21 inches (48 to 53 cm).

Eyes
Dark brown, widely spaced, gently sloping to an almond shape.

Character
Demonstrates affection toward humans. Gentle, loyal, intelligent; adaptable, alert, eager to serve, friendly but not overly aggressive. Not a pack animal; does poorly in a kennel.

The Alaskan Malamute

"Malamute" is derived from the Mahlemut Indians in northwest Alaska, who used this dog in their nomadic life.

General Appearance
Vigorous and well built, with wolflike appearance.

Coat
Thick and coarse. Dense undercoat from 1 to 2 inches (2.5 to 5 cm) long, woolly in texture. Thick fur around the neck.

Color
From light gray to black, with white on the stomach, legs, feet, and face-mask.

Size
Males, 25 inches (63.5 cm) in height, 83.6 to 86 pounds (38 to 39 kg).
Females, 23 inches (58.4 cm) in height, 72.8 to 75 pounds (33 to 34 kg).

Eyes
Brown, almond-shaped (dark eyes are preferable).

Character
Affectionate, intelligent, loyal, and friendly. Playful when invited; will never be a guard or attack dog. He is a team animal but independent. He needs firm handling, and is not a "one-man dog."

The Alaskan Husky

He belongs to a breed of sled dog considered to be the most important. With him the idea of a particular breed has somewhat disappeared. The name "Alaskan husky" is applied to northern-type dogs originating in Alaska, and does not fall into the category of registered breeds. They are selected for their speed, power, endurance, and resistance to climatic conditions. There is no standard type where they are concerned.

The Greenlander

Originating as the dog of the Eskimos of Greenland, he was the companion of the migrant hunters who left Siberia to establish themselves in Greenland. Of all the sled dogs, he is the toughest; this is the result of the merciless selection process of which he is the product.

General Appearance
Polar spitz, very strong; body is built for work and endurance.

Coat
Dense hair, straight and coarse, short on the head and paws, long on the body and underside of the tail. The undercoat is thick and soft.

Color
All colors are acceptable, solid or multicolored, with the exception of albinos.

Size
Males, 23.6 inches (60 cm).
Females, 21.6 inches (55 cm).

Eyes
Dark, slanted.

Character
Tough, well adapted to difficult conditions. He is absolutely not a house pet. Apt to run off, he quickly finds his hunting instincts when free. A pack animal, he needs authority. He is, however, amiable and sociable toward humans.

Siberian Husky

This is the race dog par excellence. He is the fastest and most beloved of the northern dogs, and is the most widespread. He originated in the northeast of Siberia, where he was raised by the Chukchis.

General Appearance
Working dog with a light, quick, and elegant gait. His balanced proportions reflect power, speed, and endurance.

Coat
The guard hairs are longer than the rest of the coat, but never extremely long. The heavy fur softens the lines of the body. The coat is neither flat against the body nor standing up. The undercoat is soft and dense.

Color
All colors are permissible.

Size
Males, 21 to 24 inches (53 to 61 cm); 45 to 62 pounds (20 to 28 kg).
Females, 20 to 22 inches (51 to 56 cm); 23 to 51 pounds (10 to 23 kg).

Eyes
Almond-shaped and gently sloping, blue in color.

Character
One of the most endearing of companions. Sociable and independent. He is a team animal, and has a strong sense of hierarchy. Playful trickster, sturdy and energetic. Almost more cat than dog.

Addresses

Alaska Dog Mushers' Association
P.O. Box 662
Fairbanks, AK 99707

Alaska Skijoring & Pulk Association
P.O. Box 82516
Fairbanks, AK 99708

Iditarod Trail Committee
P.O. Box 870800
Wasilla, AK 99687

International Sled Dog Racing Association, Inc.
1300 Reeder Creek Road
Nordman, ID 83848

John Beargrease Sled Dog Marathon
P.O. Box 500
Duluth, MN 55801

Mid-Union Sled Haulers
c/o 213 Ludwig Avenue
Battle Creek, MI 49017

Montana Sled Dog, Inc.
c/o 833 Breckenridge
Helena, MT 59601

Mushing
P.O. Box 149
Ester, AK 99725

Nenana Dog Mushers Association
c/o P.O. Box 281
Nenana, AK 99760

New England Sled Club
c/o RFD 4, Box 305B
Manchester, NH 03100

Oregon Recreational Mushers
c/o 1787 Oak Street
North Bend, OR 97459

Sierra Nevada Dog Drivers, Inc.
3991 West Peltier Road
Lodi, CA 95242

Yukon Quest International, Ltd.
P.O. Box 75015
Fairbanks, AK 99707

Photo Credits

Library of History of the National Navy/ Michel Kempf	**3, 5, 6, 7** above, **10** above, **22–23, 24** above, **38, 40, 42**
National Library	**0–1, 2** above, **8, 9, 10** below, **12, 13, 14** above, **15** above, **46** above
Bilderberg/Hans J. Burkard	**94, 95, 96** below, **97, 99, 102–103, 110, 116–117, 119, 122** below, **127** below, **136, 141** below
Jean-Louis Charmet collection	**11, 18–19, 44**
Dagli-Orti	**47**
Edimédia	**4, 7** below
Explorer/Cochin	**64** above
Explorer/A P A	**80–81**
Gamma/Isabelle Bich	**63, 66–67, 79** below, **83** above, **84–85, 86** above, **100** below, **101, 104, 105, 109** below, **111, 112** below, **115, 124–125, 126** above, **129, 132, 134, 140** below, **141** above, **142, 155** right, **156** left
Gamma/François Janin	**88**
Gamma/Michael Penn	**113** below
Dominique Grandjean	**128, 146, 147, 151, 155** left, **156** right
Francis Lacassin collection	**14** below, **15** below, **17** middle and below
Museum of Man/Michel Kempf	**2** below
Dorothy G. Page/Iditarod Trail Committee	**30, 32, 33**
Roger-Viollet	**16, 17** above, **20** above, **39, 46** below
Ivars Silis	**52, 53, 54–55, 56, 57, 58, 59, 60–61, 62, 65**
Sipa Press	**152**
Stéphane Compoint	Fly leaves, **138–139, 144–145**
Sygma diff./l'Illustration	**41, 43, 45, 48–49**
Sygma	**78** below, **78–79** above
University of Alaska, Alaska & Polar Regions Department, Hors collection	**21** above, **24** middle and below
Mrs. Henry L. Boos collection	**25** below, **27** above
Charles Bunnel collection	**28–29** above
Lanier McKee collection	**25** above
Lynn Denny collection	**20** middle
Lomen Family collection	**20** below, **21** below, **27** below, **28** middle and below, **31, 35, 36, 37**
Ralph Macky collection	**26**
Vide Bartlett collection	**34**
Wilkes collection	**29** below
Nicolas Vanier	**64** below, **68–69, 70, 71, 72, 73, 74–75, 76, 77, 82** above, **113** above
Vladimir Vinitzki	**50, 51, 82** below, **83** below, **86** below, **87, 89, 90, 91, 92–93, 96** above, **98, 100** above, **106–107, 108, 109** above, **112** above, **114, 118, 120–121, 122** above, **123, 126** below, **127** above, **130–131, 133, 135, 137, 140** above, **143, 153, 157**

If you enjoyed *Travelers of the Cold* . . .

Readers of *Travelers of the Cold: Sled Dogs of the Far North* can look to Alaska Northwest Books™ for more wilderness adventure books — from field guides to true adventure stories.

TRAPLINE TWINS
By Julie and Miki Collins

With their sled dog team, identical twins Julie and Miki Collins live a unique life in the remote Lake Minchumina region, northwest of Mount McKinley in Interior Alaska. This is their journal of adventurous wilderness living, in which dogsled, canoe, and aircraft are their transportation; and wild game, garden produce, and foraged edibles their food.

215 pages / paperback / $12.95 ($16.45 Canadian)
ISBN 0-88240-332-X

CHILKOOT PASS
The Most Famous Trail in the North
By Archie Satterfield

Experience the colorful history of the famous Chilkoot Pass, called "the meanest 32 miles in history." For the modern hiker, this is also a guide to the proper equipment, trail etiquette, and current trail conditions.

207 pages / paperback / $9.95 ($12.95 Canadian)
ISBN 0-88240-109-2

ONCE UPON AN ESKIMO TIME
By Edna Wilder

What was life like for Alaska's Eskimos in the early days? This remarkable book recounts a one-year cycle in Eskimo life, as told by a woman named Nedercook when she was 109 years old. Beautiful drawings enhance the fascinating story.

185 pages / paperback / $9.95 ($12.65 Canadian)
ISBN 0-88240-274-9

WILDERNESS SURVIVAL GUIDE
By Monty Alford

Planning is key when you're preparing for a wilderness trek in the North Country. Thirty-eight years of experience with Yukon rivers, lakes and glaciers give Monty Alford the authority to instruct you in building snow shelters, crossing icy rivers, constructing your own survival gear, and more.

104 pages / paperback / $9.95 ($12.65 Canadian)
ISBN 0-88240-317-6

ALASKA BEAR TALES and MORE ALASKA BEAR TALES
By Larry Kaniut

Anyone living or traveling in the Alaskan bush knows the ever-present danger of being attacked by a bear. These best-selling books are sometimes chilling, always gripping collections of true stories about folks who survived close calls with bears, and those who didn't.

Alaska Bear Tales / 318 pages / paperback /
$12.95 ($15.95 Canadian) / ISBN 0-88240-232-3

More Alaska Bear Tales / 295 pages / paperback /
$12.95 ($15.95 Canadian) / ISBN 0-88240-372-9

FACTS ABOUT ALASKA
The Alaska Almanac

From a complete list of Iditarod winners to the best time in the latest World Championship Sled Dog Race, this book has it all. Thousands of facts and intriguing tidbits make it the most complete reference (and trivia buff's delight) imaginable.

200 pages / paperback / $7.95 ($9.95 Canadian)
ISBN 0-88240-247-1

The MILEPOST® and The ALASKA WILDERNESS MILEPOST®

Since 1949, *The MILEPOST®* has served as the "bible of North Country travel" for travelers to Alaska and western Canada. Updated annually, this classic guide gives mile-by-mile information on what to see and do, and where to find food, gas, and lodging. It includes a fold-out "Plan-A-Trip" map and information on customs, air travel, points of interest, and visitor services. A companion guide, *The ALASKA WILDERNESS MILEPOST®* rounds out the picture with everything you need to know to discover the glories of bush Alaska (over 250 remote towns and villages covered). Look for detailed maps, color photographs, and the best information available on parks, historical sites, wildlife areas, and sporting activities (including sled dog mushing).

The MILEPOST® / 546 pages / paperback / $14.95
($18.95 Canadian) / ISBN 0-88240-214-5

The ALASKA WILDERNESS MILEPOST® / 496 pages / paperback
$14.95 ($18.95 Canadian) / ISBN 0-88240—289-7